KATERINA 'S STORY

Life in Poland During World War II and the Aftermath

A NOVEL BASED ON A TRUE EXPERIENCE

Best wishes, Carol

Lee Griffin

LEE GRIFFIN

ISBN 978-1-64003-068-8 (Paperback)
ISBN 978-1-64003-069-5 (Digital)

Covenant Books, Inc.
11661 Hwy 707
Murrells Inlet, SC 29576
www.covenantbooks.com

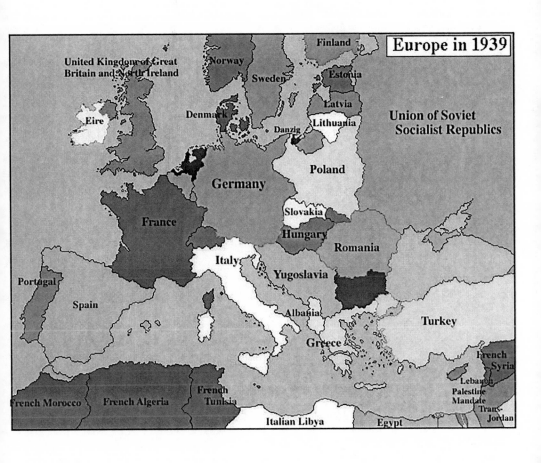

To Cathy (1923-2017) and Her Family

Childhood

Katerina

War scares me. So many young men die. My heart goes *dum dum*. I have to sit down and say a prayer because I cannot get over it. I see so much evil during World War II; I no can talk about it even to my kids. They have no interest, anyway. All I hear is "Oh, Ma, forget it. This happened a long time ago."

Even after all these years, if I see something about Hitler or the war on TV, I no can sleep worth a darn for a week. It is very painful, but my best friend, Lou Ellen, thinks my life story is worth telling and remembering. Right from the start, though, I explain to her that some things I witness are so horrible I cannot talk about them to anyone, not even her.

*   *   *

Lou Ellen

These were the words of my friend, Katerina Mandek, who was born in 1923 on a warm May morning in Horodenka, Poland. Nearby countries included Romania to the south and the Soviet Union, which lies east.

Surrounding Horodenka, which was located in the southwest corner of Poland, were forty-eight villages, most of which were built near the Dniester River. Agriculture was the area's basic economy, and most of its inhabitants worked on outlying farms where wheat, cattle, and horses were the main products. In addition to native

Polish citizens, various ethnic groups such as Ukrainians, Russians, and Jews inhabited the region.

Katerina, her parents Bruno and Sofia Mandek, and her brothers Phillip and Jakib resided in a large, two-story building that housed a doctor's office, a shoemaker, a dress shop, and a dry goods store on the ground floor. Several families occupied living quarters on the first floor.

Katerina's father was husky, six feet tall, had prickly straw hair, and pencil-sharp hazel-colored eyes. His volcanic voice erupted frequently, emitting streams of steamy curse words. A neighborhood woman found him especially desirable when he made frequent visits while dressed in his sharp army uniform and black gleaming, spit-shined boots.

Katerina's first recollection of turmoil occurred at age five, when her mother mysteriously died. As a result, her young world wavered between upsetting and topsy-turvy.

Katerina

I no learn how or why she dies. Nobody tells me a thing, but after Mother is put into the ground, a woman stranger and her four kids move into our house. Father never explains. All he says is, "This is your new stepmother, Michalina. You be nice to her, you hear me?" This is it. Nothing else. From then on, my life flips upside down, and my so-called mother pushes me away. Honestly, I no like her. She even looks mean and ugly. I still remember her long, thick granny braids coiled around her head like a snake and her crackled skin with two angry-looking slits between her eyes. Even now, I picture her face: a big brown squishy apple hiding in grass under the tree, just like the rotten fruit farmers feed to their pigs.

Michalina is skinny, tough, and as tall as Father is and copies his way of barking orders like a top dog. She hardly calls me Katerina. Instead, I am "Miss Stupid Shitski," whoever this is. I still hate these words. Just thinking about it scrambles my stomach and stirs up feelings of sadness again. Ah, well. This is life, isn't it? Anyway, it isn't long before I notice changes in my father. This is when he starts coming home from work later than ever and more often.

Lou Ellen

When Michalina nagged Katerina's father for an explanation of his frequent tardiness, Bruno explained that important business at the army post required him to stay there until he solved a pressing problem. "You lie," Michalina shouted. "I don't believe you. Are you chasing skirts?" Then her father exploded, Katerina recalled, and another argument snapped and crackled. Katerina said she ran to her bedroom and finger-plugged her ears.

Katerina

This is when my father do no smiles, plays games, or even jokes with Phillip and me anymore. He is angry or upset nearly every day. I do not understand why.

When my stepmother's kids break toys or knickknacks, I catch the blame, and she hauls off and smacks me. Then when Father comes home from the post, she tells lies, and he believes her, not me. Do you know how hurtful this is for a kid? At the same time, I am confused, and my heart feels like it will split wide open. Even so, I no can say a word. If I do, she will get even with me later.

With her kids, it is a different story. The oldest girl, Pepi, who is almost twelve, never dusts or picks up after herself, her sister, or her two brothers. When the little boys finish playing, they leave blocks, cars, trucks, and toy soldiers scattered all over the floor. Phillip and I go to another room to be by ourselves. He always paints or draws and usually starts in on a puzzle or reads a favorite book. Just when we are enjoying the peace and quiet, my stepmother comes in the room with both hands on her hips and gives us the eagle eye. "Listen, stupid shit," she says. "It is time you and your brother get to work. Phillip, you can muck out the cow barn. And you, girl, you've got dusting, sweeping steps, and washing dishes. You both can handle that, can't you? Wait. Before you begin, I want you to pick all the toys scattered on the floor and put in the proper place. Get it?"

Yeah, I get it. This is not fair. Phillip and I picked up already. Her kids should take care of their own mess. Hoping Michalina will calm down, I tame my tongue and do not sass or argue. While she stands there waiting, I do as I am told and start picking up her kids' toys and put them away. Phillip, though, sits like a frog on a log sunning himself and doesn't move. Instead, he scrunches up his face and flips a thick strand of dark hair away from his forehead. Next, he flashes his cocky face. "No," he shouts at the top of his voice, "do it yourself, you bitch!"

Suddenly, my brother has enough sense to stop. Even so, I think, *Oh, boy. You are in deep trouble now, and you better watch out.* Well, Michalina rushes over to slap him, but I step in front, and she wallops me across the cheek. This stings like a mad hornet, but I hang tough and shed not a single teardrop.

Phillip rushes out of the room, hollering, "You just wait. I'm going to tell Father on you." And her answer? "Go ahead, boy. You do, and I'll beat your ass good."

It hurts that Father does nothing, but then, Michalina is his queen. At night when they think I am sleeping, I hear them talking about what my father says is getting hitched. Now Michalina yells, calling Father a jerk, "Are you too good to say 'married' Bruno? Horses are hitched, you idiot." He half laughs then turns serious. I hear only parts of what they say. It is something about the priest who will not marry them. "Forget him," Father says, "and forget marriage. Let's not rush into this, okay? We don't need that priest, anyway, do we, babe?"

*　　*　　*

Lou Ellen

In the months ahead, Katerina recalled that she continued weathering her stepmother's verbal and physical abuse, as well as her father's indifference. During that period, a bevy of civil childhood authorities and Catholic church officials responded to neighbor complaints as fights and arguments between Bruno and Michalina intensified. Finally, the Sisters of Nazareth took a bewildered Katerina from her home, and she began life at the nearby convent with several other abused children and orphans. It was there that Sister Mary Elizabeth took a shy and fearful girl under her wing. She explained the rules and regulations Katerina must follow. She also listed the duties and responsibilities of all the children residing at the convent. She assured Katerina not to be frightened, that "everything will work out fine. You will be happy here in no time."

During the day, Katerina noted, she and the other convent children attended the Polish government school in Horodenka. The student population consisted of Jewish, Polish, and Ukrainian children. As was common the in early 1930s, kindergarten class did not exist. Boys and girls began first grade at age six and attended classes through the sixth grade. The sexes were educated separately in different buildings, with the boy's school at one end of town near the sports arena. The girl's facility was located outside the city center.

Jewish parents who lived in Horodenka sent their children half day to the government school where they studied basic subjects such as reading, writing, and numbers. Afternoons were spent at the Jewish school while students took classes in Hebrew language, history, and religion.

Katerina

In our government school, we sometimes have two classes for each grade. That's because many kids work on the farms. They still have to spend part of the time in school, though. A few people who live in Horodenka own farmland, but it is five or six miles away from their homes. Many foreigners like Russian or Ukrainian families work the land for the owners.

My grandmother owns a farm away from the city, but she lives there and hires workers to tend the crops and animals. She often tells me that I will own the place someday because Polish law says so.

* * *

Lou Ellen

Katerina went on to explain how she first came to live with the nuns at the convent. She noted that although more than fifty decades have passed, time has not diminished her memory. She recalled a private conversation she had with Sister Mary Elizabeth and said she could recall the nun's words practically word for word.

The episode began when the nun asked Katerina how her schoolwork was progressing. "Fine," she assured Sister Mary, who then switched the subject to her late mother. "Dear child. Are you aware I knew your mother very well? She was a kind, thoughtful woman—and very beautiful. She told me many things about herself and family. When you grow older, I will explain matters that you may not understand at this point in your life. Nevertheless, what you need to know is that just before your mother passed, she told me how much she loved you and your brother. Always remember that she will continue loving and watching over you two forever. Never ever forget this, my dear."

At first, Katerina said she was speechless. Then she thought perhaps there actually was hope for future happiness in her life. Maybe it was possible that she was not a worthless stupid shit after all. She stared at Sister Mary's creamy face and recalled her honey-like voice slathering syrupy words across her eardrums with much care and kindness. Katerina was so touched, she said, that she had to suppress a persistent urge to break out sobbing.

Katerina

When I hear this, I make two promises: one to myself and one to God. Someday I will take all the vows and become a nun. My permanent home will be the convent, and I will live in peace and harmony with my loving sisters. When I am a grown-up, I hope and pray people will say, "Praise be! You are exactly like Sister Mary Elizabeth. Is she your twin sister?"

Lou Ellen

After several months of convent living, and as Katerina gradually adjusted to cloistered life, she learned from the sisters that her father was negotiating with the mother superior in an effort to bring her back home.

Katerina

I come back from school to the convent one day when Father is there. He is looking spiffy in his brown jacket, creased khaki pants, and spit-shined boots. He is talking to one of the sisters. When I come over, he pats my shoulder and says, "Katerina has been here almost six months now. It is time she comes back home. Her brother misses her and...we all do. I promise Mother Superior that I will meet all her demands."

Lou Ellen

As my friend described it, those promises rolled off her father's tongue like water. Holy Mother's demands included no physical abuse from Michalina as well no more cursing and name-calling. Household chores had to be equally distributed among all the children, and every family member must attend mass regularly.

Katerina

I don't believe my father. Here he is, practically down on his knees, begging for forgiveness. Repeatedly, he claims, "I will make everything right. Just give me another chance. I dearly love my little girl, I really do."

Lou Ellen

Obviously, the fact that her father sucked up to Mother Superior and the Sisters of Nazareth was a success because a few days later, Katerina said she landed back home. She doubted if her father really understood her feelings.

As for her stepmother, Katerina said, "That scruffy she-dog can bark up a tree as far as I am concerned. She will never change."

Katerina

I don't remember how long I am treated halfway decent, but Father takes us to mass for a couple of weeks. Michalina refuses and stays home. Before long, she pushes me hard. "Go feed the animals and clean out their shit. Sweep these steps, scrub this dirty floor, and get your little ass to the river and wash these diapers." Do this. Do that. It never ends.

All the while, Michalina's lazy daughter, Pepi, laughs at me. During this time, Sister Mary Elizabeth makes her regular neighborhood visits checking on the old and sick people. Well, she comes to our next-door neighbor and gives him food and medicine. Later, she stops by our place. I am outside cleaning the stall where the animals are kept, and Sister says, "Child, what is it you are doing?" I explain that Michalina gives me this job, and I better get cracking or she will beat me. "Look, Sister Mary," I say, while I bend over so she can see the top of my head. "See how much hair she pulls out."

"What?" Sister's eyes get big as saucers. "Oh, dear God, Mary mother of Jesus," she says, leaving me and hurrying indoors. I have no idea what she says to my stepmother, but I hear yelling and screaming. I stay put. After Sister Mary leaves, Michalina comes stomping outdoors and chews me out. "You get your miserable skinny ass inside, right this minute!" she yells, turning back and opening the door. I keep working. I do not want her touching me. In a few minutes, she comes to the door, again, and hollers, "Did you tell that nun all of our business? No? Then who in hell does she think she is, telling me what I should do? The pope?"

Lou Ellen

Later, when Katerina's father came home from work, Michalina fudged her side of the story. Bruno then asked his daughter if she did in fact ask Sister to stop and visit. "No, I didn't," she answered.

"But Michalina said you did." Again, Katerina claimed her innocence.

"She is telling you lies, Father."

He boiled over. His face flushed crimson, and he yelled at the top of his voice. "I believe your stepmother. Drop it."

Still fresh in her memory were the denials, screaming, yelling, and swearing—commotion that prompted the next-door neighbor barging through the door. The woman chided her father. "Listen, Bruno," she reminded him, "I heard every word you said. Why don't you believe your daughter? She had nothing to do with Sister Mary Elizabeth's visit. Sister came to our place first bringing my husband his medicine and changing the bandage on his arm. If you cannot settle your differences, I will call the police."

Katerina

Our nice neighbor shakes her finger at my stepmother and warns, "You, Michalina, will die a very bad death because you lie and mistreat Katerina very badly."

Oh, wow! Father does not like hearing this, and he shouts, "This is none of your damn business. Get out of my house—right now!"

Our neighbor fires back. "This is your house? Who do you think you are fooling? This is your daughter Katerina's place. It does not belong to you. Not only that, I will come and go as I please, just as I did when your lovely wife was alive, God rest her soul."

That settles it. Father doesn't argue with her or say another word. He knows it is the truth.

*   *   *

Lou Ellen

Back in those days, Katerina explained, it was her understanding that Polish law dictated that when her widowed grandmother passed away, Katerina's birth mother became the rightful owner of the family dwellings and land. However, since Katerina's mother predeceased her own mother, Katerina and any living siblings would become legal owners of the farmhouse and land as well as the place in Horodenka.

Katerina

When my neighbor reminds Father that I will own the property and houses someday, I see myself living in my own place on a chilly night. After fixing a light meal, I sit and relax in the front room with a purring tabby in my lap, all without a care in the world. Next, I picture big brother Phillip living out of town in his farmhouse studio, painting and drawing up a storm. As a popular artist, his work sells so well; his hired hands and trusted manager operates the entire farm, overseeing the animals, land, and…Quick as a flash, my dreaming stops. I cannot help but wonder if any part of this fantasy will come true.

Lou Ellen

For the most part, Katerina was tired of her yo-yo, up-and-down family life—the okay days and those filled with anger and conflict. Nevertheless, the thirteen-year-old persevered, but she was unhappy with her looks. She described herself as reed thin and short. Red pimples dotted her pale forehead and chin. Her schoolmates' skin looked the same. However, the teen believed that beauty evolved with age. She witnessed shy and homely neighborhood girls her age turn into graceful attractive young women when they reached age sixteen or seventeen. However, Katerina's plain-Jane appearance belied her growing inner strength and resiliency as evidenced in flare-ups with her parents.

Katerina

I am in the middle of second semester at school when Michalina starts harping, demanding that I do all these chores: washing her little kids' diapers, washing and putting away dishes, making beds, and sweeping the steps before and after school. She is crazy as an outhouse rat. "Hell will freeze two times over before I will do all this," I scream. "You have a daughter who can work a little, and so can you!" Then I rush off and head out for school.

Lou Ellen

When Katerina's father returned home from work, and Michalina informed him about the fiery argument she had with his daughter, he jumped all over Katerina, intending to intimidate her. Instead, his tirade had the opposite effect. Just as a spark and dry tinder can induce flame, Katerina's smoldering temper suddenly flared up into a blazing fire. She demanded an answer.

Katerina

I ask him, "Am I your servant? Or some dumb Dora you pull off the street?"

"No, don't be silly. You are my daughter," my father says.

I sass him back. "I don't think so. Pepi is your daughter. I am just a poor servant girl in my own house."

"No," he argues. "This is not true. You are either exaggerating or making it all up. Are you crazy?"

I try to make him understand. "Father, listen to me. I cannot possibly do all the chores she gives me. As it is—"

Father raises his fist but suddenly drops it. I go on explaining that I have no free time after school for hanging out with classmates or doing extra schoolwork. Michalina keeps a list of chores for me to do, and I am always rushing home. "Do you know how it feels not having any friends?" Father is silent. Our talk is going nowhere, so I give up. He stares me down. Suddenly, out of nowhere, I throw a dart and hope it hits. "Oh, by the way, Father. Why are you ignoring your promises to Mother Superior and the sisters, huh? You are breaking your word of honor, do you realize this, or don't you care?"

By now, Michalina butts in, shooting off her mouth from the kitchen. "You better shut your trap right now." Father gets up and goes into the kitchen. She keeps quiet after that, but Pepi barges in with a warning. "You just wait. When your Father leaves, my mother will switch your legs until you beg her to stop. You'll see."

I always wonder whether people like Michalina and Pepi are in some way ever paid back for the terrible way they treat people. I believe they are, and I remind Pepi that her life might give her a few problems she will have to solve, which she should think about, and maybe "your rotten attitude will change." Well, she brushes me off and ignores my suggestion. Then she curls her lip, turns her back, and takes off.

Now what I say next sounds crazy, but I swear this is the truth. A few years later, Pepi develops swelling under both eyes that resembles large lima beans planted under her skin. Michalina takes her to just about every doctor in Horodenka to find out if she has some disease, or if there is a treatment for her condition. As I recall, no doctor can offer a solution, which makes both mother and daughter meaner and uglier. Maybe they are receiving their due after all. I like to think so. I hope so.

* * *

Lou Ellen

Subsequently, the Sisters of Nazareth intervened once again, and Katerina reentered the convent. Neither the nuns nor Mother Superior offered Katerina any information regarding the length of her stay.

Katerina

I am sure that Sister Mary Elizabeth talked with Mother Superior about me coming back. Between them and the child welfare people, I believe they want me living here at the convent until I grow up and am on my own.

Lou Ellen

According to Katerina, in the beginning, she chafed under the strict convent rules and the ever-watchful eyes of Sister Mary Elizabeth and the other nuns. However, the headstrong teen soon learned her life was much easier and less stressful if she cooperated. Before long, she made a conscious effort to follow rules without questioning their importance. She recalled that she tried being good but was always concerned about doing something wrong and making mistakes.

Katerina

I worry that the sisters will get tired of putting up with me and send me back home. They tell me it will never happen. When I hear this, it is like magic. I suddenly feel light and airy, with my heart fluttering like a butterfly.

Lou Ellen

The teenager attended classes at the government school until late afternoon, and then she returned to the cloister. She enjoyed a short fruit or cookie break with the others and then buckled down with an older nun who made certain she completed her school assignments. If Katerina needed help with other homework, the same nun assisted her.

Katerina

Here I am always busy and very happy. The convent is so different from home: no yelling, screaming or swearing, no fighting with Father or Michalina and her kids, and no shoving, pushing, or beatings. The only person I really miss is my brother, Phillip. Sister Mary Elizabeth tells me he is attending the boy's military academy on a government grant and is living away from home. I am happy for him. Maybe the good Lord will take care of us from now on.

* * *

Lou Ellen

The convent interior featured two wings, one of which housed, at various times, five to a dozen abused and orphaned children. They resided in dormitories, each grouped according to age. In addition to a separate section for the nuns, there was a service wing, which included a kitchen, dining facilities, storage areas, offices, and a chapel.

Mother Superior headed the convent staff and made important decisions. Her nuns carried out administrative duties, supervised the kitchen, tended the vegetable garden, and managed other facilities.

Katerina's day began when all the children woke up around 6:00 a.m. They dressed and then attended mass in the chapel. Following mass, which ended at 7:00 a.m., the youngsters washed up for breakfast. In the dining hall, the breakfast was oatmeal or another cooked cereal, fruit (usually an apple), a slice of bread with butter, if available, and a glass of milk.

Katerina

After breakfast, we make up our cots and clean the room. We sweep and wash the cement floor. If we don't do this, the room gets awfully dusty. If anybody has dirty laundry, he throws it in the corner. If it's a big pile, you are supposed to wash and rinse the clothes by hand and then hang them indoors on clotheslines. In nice weather, everything goes outdoors.

It seems to me we study all the time, even when we don't attend school on the weekends or on certain holidays. Then various nuns give us Bible lessons, plus reading and writing assignments anyway. Certain nuns work only with kids who have trouble with arithmetic. Most of them have a terrible time with story problems. Like I say, when regular school is out, we study and work here on homework between 9:00 a.m. and noon. If us older kids finish our assignments early, we work with the younger boys and girls who need extra help.

Lou Ellen

Lunch, cleaning up, and washing dishes occurred between 12:30 and 1:30 or 2:00 p.m. The usual fare was soup and sandwich, or egg on toast and a piece of fruit.

Katerina

The boys and girls, who are between eight and ten years old, take turns washing and drying the dishes, while the kids my age work in the garden out back. We hoe weeds and collect vegetables for supper. We pick carrots, onions, and lettuce. When the beets are big, we pick them too. The cooks get all excited when we bring them beets because they love making borscht. If they have leftover pieces of meat or bones, they throw it all in the pot, along with anything else they can find. When one of the cooks serves us borscht, her favorite saying is, "This is the best borscht yet. Everything is in it except the kitchen sink. Let me know if anyone finds a little creature swimming around in it." Right away, the kids squeal, and the nuns moan. She is always kidding around and likes having fun.

Sisters do not allow five-year-old kids or younger anywhere in the garden. At first, some children help nuns pull weeds, but before long, the job becomes boring, and they take off and run up and down the rows. In their excitement, they end up tramping all over the plants. Still, they pout and pester the sisters with, "Please, can we go in the garden today? We will not run, and we will watch where we walk. Can we, please? Oh, you never let us do anything that is fun."

Lou Ellen

Several times a week, boys and girls enjoyed a break from chores or homework when occasional afternoons were devoted to arts and crafts. Girls who were near Katerina's age fashioned coasters, knitted scarves, and small articles of clothing. In addition, a few girls skilled in crocheting and embroidery contributed baby and household items. Then, once a year, the sisters offered the accumulated goods for sale to the public.

Katerina

Making felt and cloth coasters are my favorite activity. Once the pieces are trimmed square and sewn together, the edges are ready for fancy needlework. Next, the nun in charge comes around and checks to see if the coasters look good enough to sell. She is the elderly sister whose crinkly face makes her look crabby, but she is one of the nicest around. While we are working on our projects, she needs to sit down often, and when standing or walking, Sister uses her cane. Even so, you can tell she enjoys helping us. I enjoy sitting next to her so I can ask questions about sewing or anything else that pops into my mind. When the craft session ends, she has a sweet way of purring in her tiny voice, saying, "My big and little lambkins, everything here looks perfect. You all did a very good job."

Boys, on the other hand, do not bother with sewing; most enjoy carving wooden toys and figures or painting designs on bottles and containers.

Everyone at the convent and our Polish neighbors look forward every summer to our outdoor annual arts and crafts shows. With lots of handmade stuff to choose from at good prices, we attract a good turnout from Horodenka residents and out-of-town people.

Sets of four coasters cost two zloty (two dollars) each. They are popular and sell out fast. Winter scarves, baby blankets, hats, and other knitted pieces bring higher prices, but they are snapped up quickly too. At day's end, everyone seems happy: the buyers, the children, the Sisters of Nazareth, and Mother Superior. All proceeds are used to meet convent needs, which include basic food items, clothing for children and the sisters, convent repair and maintenance, mission work, neighborhood outreach projects, and craft supplies.

Lou Ellen

Prior to supper time, monastery children performed rotating chores, such as picking up trash or papers around the yard or gathering small sticks and twigs, then stacking them in piles for use as fireplace kindling. In addition, they took turns sweeping hallways and outside entrances with willow brooms. Most jobs were performed willingly, as the youngsters believed Sister Mary Elizabeth's often repeated observation that "cleanliness is the next best thing to godliness, and we want this for every one of you."

Suppertime took place in the dining hall between 6:30 and 7:00 p.m. The food consisted of various salads, toasted sandwiches, and since the sisters raised laying hens, poached eggs. Individual meat servings rarely found their way to the table. Instead, small pork or beef pieces combined with various vegetables made tasty stews, soups, and pasta dishes. Everyone, including youngsters, workers, nuns, and Mother Superior, shared the same diet.

The nuns ruled their charges with an iron fist, noted Katerina. They had no tolerance for disobedience, lying, willfulness, and other such behavior. Every individual had to behave within reason. Children requiring behavior correction were usually hustled to the nearest corner facing the wall.

Katerina

When it finally sinks into a kid's head that he cannot get away with bad behavior, and everyone around him is playing and otherwise having fun, young "corner kids" as the sisters call them, blubber their heads off. Older boys and girls stand quietly with their heads bowed, as they shift their weight from one foot to the other. While the punishment is not that hard, most children act so sad and lonely that I cannot help but feel sorry for them. As a rule, one time in the corner is enough for most kids, and they learn proper behavior in quick order.

Occasionally, there are exceptions, but these youngsters are troubled or beyond repair so they are placed somewhere else, I guess; they do not stay here very long.

I consider myself very lucky for escaping time in the corner. I came too close for comfort, though. You see, one sister jumped all over me for being sassy. Well, she kept harping about it. When I am finally sick of hearing it, out of my mouth pops, "Oh, please, Sister. Be quiet and do your job." In a flash, she threatens to scrub my mouth out with a bar of laundry soap. She flies at me as though she will jam it down my throat. I push further and announce, "Hey, here I am, Sister. Go ahead and try." In an instant, hurt curdles her face. Suddenly, she whips around and walks away, leaving me alone and regretting my words. All day I feel like beating myself silly. I do not understand how I can lower myself by disrespecting a kind and caring nun who rescues me from a living hell. How dare I, a snotty-nosed kid, forget my place and talk back to a good adult? Much later, I finally get up enough nerve, go to Sister, and tell her how sorry I am for hurting her and acting so stupid. "Katerina, child, I forgive you," Sister says, throwing her arms around me. "Erase it from your mind. I have." My goodness. This was so long ago. Even today, her words bring back an early memory of a dog ripping meat from a bone and wishing I could cork my eyes and stop the heavy flow.

Lou Ellen

Throughout that incident, Katerina related that she could not help but compare the nun's response to her scornful retort with similar experiences she had with Michalina. In the latter case, Katerina's cocky attitude guaranteed that she would receive both physical and verbal abuse from her stepmother. At that moment, my friend noted, she vowed that she would never return home under any circumstances because home ceased to exist following her mother's death. Even the Sisters of Nazareth discouraged her from doing so.

Katerina

Sister Mary warns me, saying, "If you do go home, you probably will not come back. The last time we take you from your stepmother, I must grab her hair and twist since she refuses to let you leave. If you go back now, she will get even with you and probably beat you silly. Then your father will turn against me, get mad, and swear like a drunken sailor. I no longer care to deal with either one."

I explain to Sister that I miss my brother, Phillip, very much. "He is away at military school and will join the Polish army when he graduates." I really believe my brother is a smart kid for leaving home once he received the government scholarship. He and Father did not get along, and he absolutely could not stand Michalina.

Lou Ellen

Sister Mary Elizabeth informed Katerina, who was then a teenager, that her charge was "putting the cart before the horse" unnecessarily. When the time came, Sister assured her, she would enlist the aid of Mother Superior for arranging many opportunities for sibling visits at the convent. The nun then asked Katerina if she remembered that she promised they would chat about "your beautiful mother, Sofia, and now that you are approaching maturity, we will talk."

Katerina

Sister Mary Elizabeth reveals that my mother describes our family life and hints that her account may embarrass or sicken me. Still, she believes I deserve to learn the truth and says she is confident that I am strong enough to accept the facts no matter how unpleasant. Sister then invites me to join her in the small room adjacent to the dining hall after supper.

Lou Ellen

That meeting, occurring so long ago, made such an impression on Katerina; she described the room and Sister's revelations in detail.

Katerina acknowledged the two met the same night in a sparsely furnished side room, with herself and Sister Mary sitting in heavy oak chairs facing each other across a matching table. The sister wasted no time with small talk. She came directly to the point, saying, "I want you to know how sorry I am that your mother passed away at such a young age. She was a lovely woman. We had many long talks here at the convent, or at your home when I was making my weekly neighborhood visits. We quickly became good friends. No one knew what caused her death. Authorities finally concluded that the probable cause was that she ingested poisonous mushrooms. Apparently, no one else in your family ate them. I do know she was fond of walking in the woods foraging for mushrooms, greens, and berries.

"Your mother may have died of poisoning, Katerina, but in my opinion, I think she also died of a broken heart. She shed tears when she explained she had another son who passed some years ago, and she agonized over the trouble she was having with your father. As you know, when your mother died, Michalina and her kids quickly moved in. The rest I am going to tell you is shameful and disgusting, but not one word is gossip. Unfortunately, this is the gospel truth, straight from the lips of our parish priest. Do you have any questions, so far?"

Stunned beyond words, Katerina said she sat silent and wondered what was coming next.

Katerina

At first, Sister Mary stumbles along, saying, "Hmmm, let me see. How shall I put this more delicately?" It seems like forever before she begins speaking. Her silence is very awkward. Finally, her words bolt as a runaway horse. "First, your father asks Father Sikorski to perform the sacrament of matrimony between him and Michalina— the nerve of him," she added. "He then describes her as being a long-time neighborhood friend. At the end of their conversation, Reverend Father explains that under no circumstances can he perform the ceremony. In the first place, Father Sikorski explains that Michalina is your father's first cousin, and such a marriage is unlawful. Secondly, your father admits under questioning that he did sire several of her children while married to your dear mother. With that revelation, your father curses and shouts that the Reverend Father can 'stick it where the sun doesn't shine' and that Michalina is his first love, and still is. He then puts up a bold front and says he doesn't need or want Father Sikorski's blessing, anyway."

Now for the first time, everything Sister Mary tells me makes sense: Father coming home from the post late so often and blaming his work when he is fooling around with his "first love" and the reason the two cannot marry. It serves him right. His behavior toward my mother is disgusting and embarrassing. At that moment, I lose all respect for my father. He makes me sick.

Lou Ellen

My friend continued filling me in with more details and went on. She said Sister Mary looked across at her while she kept her head bowed. She was staring at a black scuffmark on the front chair leg, feeling sad and lonely. Sister Mary Elizabeth asked her softly, "Is there anything you want to say? Do you have any questions you want to ask?" Katerina shook her head. She debated with herself whether she should uncover the secret she kept buried for a long, long time. Katerina admitted she hesitated several times and then said, "Sister Mary, I think it is time I tell you something."

Katerina

Back then, Jakib is twelve or thirteen, I remember. This all takes place when I am seven or eight years old, just before the Sisters of Nazareth take me into the convent for the first time.

Well, for as long as I can remember, Father rags on Jakib because he hardly ever enjoys playing outdoors and shies away from joining other boys for sports or just having fun. Instead, he likes doing things by himself. On one particular day, my brother stays indoors all day long. Suddenly, I hear Father's voice. He is swearing and yelling. "Get outdoors," he hollers. "Right this minute! Do not let me catch you in this house again or you are going to be one sorry son of a bitch."

Sometime later, when my brother thinks it is safe, he goes back to his drawing project. Father happens to come home early and finds him indoors again. I get scared, so I run to my room and block my ears. Before long, I hear scraping across the floor, crashing furniture, Jakib crying, and Father screaming like a mad monkey. "Why don't you play ball and roughhouse like other boys? I know why. You are nothing but a big-ass sissy, that's why. You had better start acting like a man, or you'll be about as popular as a dog turd. Do you understand?" All the while, Father is beating Jakib's butt with a leather razor strap. That night, I hear Jakib sniffling and crying softly. The next morning, he does not wake up. After that, everything is a blur: the doctor from downstairs coming up, officials asking questions, the funeral, and afterward, my pain, helplessness, and the constant warnings from Father and Michalina to "say nothing to nobody." I am afraid and worried. What will happen next?

After telling everything to Sister, in between wiping my eyes and blowing my nose, I admit how heartsick I still am that my oldest brother didn't stand a chance for making his dream come true. I remind Sister that art was Jakib's special gift, but his death killed any chance for him to develop into a successful artist.

I recall Sister Mary Elizabeth saying to me, "Oh, you poor child. I am so sorry for all that has happened, but you must go on with life and look ahead to better times."

Lou Ellen

In addition, Sister Mary told the teen that while she too regretted that Katerina's brother did not live long enough to reach his full potential, Katerina "most definitely would."

Katerina

I press Sister Mary. "How?" I am curious. "Well," she says, "Mother Superior and the sisters have high expectations and plans for you, my dear."

"What are the plans and expectations?"

She puts me off. "Not now, my child. In time, you will learn everything you need to know. You have a very bright future ahead of you, girl."

Lou Ellen

For the first time within recent memory, Katerina believed that the convent would remain her permanent home. Not only was she safe from harm there, she was also valued as an individual. Furthermore,

Katerina said she was thrilled that the nuns were confident of her future success but wondered why they were withholding details.

Katerina

If their plans are for me to study hard, take the vows, become a nun, and live in the convent forever, I will do it. Teaching little orphans suits me too. I can even nurse the sick with lots of study and training. Who knows? Time will decide.

Hospital

Lou Ellen

Within a few weeks, Katerina began her job at Horodenka's Catholic Hospital, which was located several blocks away from the convent. Sister Mary Elizabeth encouraged her to listen carefully to the sisters who operate the facility. "They will act as your teachers and advisors," she said. "Learn as much from them as you can."

Katerina

Even Mother Superior expects a lot from me and says she wants me to become a nurse or a midwife. A midwife in Horodenka is much respected and very busy. Pregnant women do not enter hospitals to have their babies. They give birth at home with help from midwives. I am so excited when I think about becoming a nurse or midwife, I can feel my heart thumping inside my chest.

Lou Ellen

Other teenagers, besides Katerina who live at the cloister, also worked at the hospital. When public school was in in session, they labored only on weekends. During the summer, the group worked three or four days a week.

Katerina

All of us walk together from the convent to the hospital. Once we are there, the head nun assigns us jobs. The different chores are washing dishes, scrubbing floors, bringing fresh water to patients, carrying food trays to their rooms, weeding flower beds, and if you are lucky like me, working with babies and little kids. I love giving the babies their baths, toweling them dry, and smoothing the silky sweet-smelling powder all over their soft skins. Then I give them their bottles, change their diapers, and rock them so they will not cry for their mommas. When I dress the little ones in gowns or shirts and diapers, I wrap them in blankets. Then I cuddle with them, coo, and make funny noises with my lips. A few babies answer with smiles, and some even light up their eyes. I am here to make them comfortable and give them love. I do my best. Do you know what happens next? Well, when I watch these young ones perk up, I melt like hot butter. Suddenly, all the bad memories from home fade away; it is amazing.

Lou Ellen

The hospital complex consisted of four large brick buildings surrounded by a large garden and play areas. The equipment included swings, slides, a merry-go-round, and climbing apparatus. Older children played kickball, soccer, and other games in large open spaces comprising the facility.

Katerina

When I take the little kids outdoors for a stroll or to the play area, I tie knots in a long, heavy rope two feet apart. One end goes around my waist. You see, the knots make it easier for toddlers to hang on to the rope. It is a hospital rule that all leaders like me have to follow, so I am very strict with the kids. If I feel the rope go slack, I ask them who is taking his hand off the rope. When I learn who the culprit is, I march us back inside the hospital. Everyone moans and groans knowing that their chance for playing games, running, and having fun is gone.

To tell the truth, I am as happy as a duck in water doing this job. Growing up at home, playing and having fun never happens. I only remember washing dishes and diapers, cleaning the house and doing most chores, while Michalina's lazy daughter Pepi doesn't have to lift a finger. It still burns me up when I think about it.

When I work at the hospital, I earn ten zloty (ten dollars) a week, which I give to the convent. I never keep the money for myself because I do not need it. Just as long as the Sisters of Nazareth feed me and give me a place to stay, they should have whatever amount I earn. If I need socks, underwear, or clothes, the nuns buy them for me. I also help the nuns work in the vegetable and flower gardens. I enjoy working with my hands very much.

Lou Ellen

According to war records, documents, and other historical material I have pursued over time, it was evident that Poland's political upheaval and its poor economy made life very difficult for individuals and families. For the most part, the Catholic Church was no exception. Money was tight. The sisters constantly searched for ways and means to secure enough food to keep the convent residents from starving.

Katerina noted that there was a kind, generous farmer living nearby who offered to help the sisters out. He promised Mother Superior he would grow extra produce for the convent. In addition, he encouraged the nuns to help themselves to both unpicked apples and pears on his trees as well as the drops littering the ground.

Katerina

In the fall, when it is the proper time to dig potatoes, several nuns and three or four of us older kids visit the farmer. We say to him, "Hey, Grandpa. Is there anything we can have in your fields or on the ground today?" He answers, "Yah, yah. Go see. I must till the soil and plant winter wheat today. Thank heaven, today is my happy day. I have sisters, young bucks, and fillies today." Actually, Grandpa is somebody you don't forget. He laughs and pats his big overhanging belly. He twirls and prances up and down every time we visit. He looks a hundred years old, like Father Time with his long milkweed, fluff-like beard and mustache. Sweat beads drop from beneath his floppy hat. He pecks at least one girl on the cheek, laughs, and in a fake sad voice, says, "Oh, you give me such a little bitty kiss. Give me a great big smacker." Just before each trip to the farm, the nuns remind us, "Grandpa is an old man and doesn't realize what he is saying, so just act nice."

Lou Ellen

At times, the nuns and their helpers dug four or five heaping bushels of potatoes and carrots. In addition, they loaded up on cabbages, beets, onions, and turnips. All fruit and berries they managed to gather in season were considered special treats.

Katerina

When we finish digging potatoes and gathering other vegetables, we pick apples and pears off the ground. When that work is over, Grandpa lifts the heavy baskets up and into his cart, hitches up the horse, and hauls everything back to the convent.

Produce is stored in the convent cellar, which retains an average temperature of thirty-five to forty degrees Fahrenheit year around. Most vegetables that are stored correctly, and oftentimes inspected, will last from four to six months.

Sisters and those of us who are helpers carry bushel baskets of potatoes to one section of the dirt floor on wooden pallets while others cover the carrots and other root vegetables with damp sand in another area. Apples and some fruits give off a type of gas that causes potato spoilage, so workers store them in a corner far away. Certain nuns have the responsibility to inspect the produce every day and keep track of the humidity. If the air becomes very dry, the vegetables and fruit will shrivel. During an inspection, if anyone spots a brown spot or signs of beginning rot, the affected fruits or vegetables are removed immediately. As a result, the defective produce winds up in the kitchen. The cooks are experts at using the good parts to make unusual mixed vegetables, various sauces, and other fruity desserts for the residents. Even so, nearly everything they create is very tasty.

*　　*　　*

Lou Ellen

Katerina described her sixteenth-birthday celebration in the cloister as a complete surprise. No one knew the reason Mother Superior was making a rare appearance following the evening meal, but everyone assumed she was announcing bad news. Instead, the Reverend Mother informed the gathering that "we're going to have a fun party, and Sister Mary Elizabeth will begin the celebration."

Katerina

After the dishes are cleared and set aside, Sister Mary makes me stand up while the whole room breaks out singing the birthday song. Then comes the special treat: little chocolate cakes with few pieces of dried fruit. Each person receives one, but mine shows up with seven pink candles on top, one on the left, and six others bunched on the right. By now, I'm feeling like a queen but at the same time embarrassed. I feel the red color of my cheeks and forehead. It gets worse when several nuns make flattering remarks about my character, using words like *kind, honest, strong, responsible,* and *hardworking.* Then Mother Superior says, "Listen, children. Katerina first comes here as a frightened little, skinny girl. Today, she is a beautiful sixteen-year-old young woman—a little willful at times and still a bit thin. We are still working on that!" Everyone laughs and claps. Bucky, a boy my age or a little younger, stands up and says, "Mother Superior, I have a funny birthday joke. Can I tell it? Please?" Boys and girls roar in approval.

At first, Mother Superior frowns. She hesitates for a second. Then I guess she figures she has no choice, so she gives in. "Go ahead, son," she says, "but it better be a good one." He promises holy Mother that his joke is a winner, hitches up his trousers, and begins: "Does anybody here know how the bunny rabbit's birthday turns out?" The room stays quiet as a dead mouse. He urges the group to guess. Again, there is silence. Bucky rolls his eyes. "No guesses? Well, he has a hoppy one! Get it?" There is so much moaning and groaning, I feel sorry and a little bit embarrassed for him. Mother Superior hushes everyone, thanks him for sharing, and says, "Let's get back to our birthday girl. I want all of you to remember my words. I have no doubt that in a few years down the road, this young person, Katerina, will become a Sister of Nazareth and live here in the convent. Do you not agree, Sister Mary Elizabeth?" Sister Mary nods and adds, "However, if this is not her choice, I am certain Katerina will bring babies into the world as a midwife."

When the party ends, I am speechless. All I can say is, "Wow. Thank you for everything. This is something I will never forget, ever."

*   *   *

Lou Ellen

At this period in her life, Katerina emphasized she was confident she would have a bright future. She described the convent as her first real home, filled with kind and loving family members. In addition, she also pointed out that she had a most enjoyable and satisfying job at the hospital. Her work was never boring but always interesting. She was constantly learning and perfecting various skills at the hospital and convent.

Katerina

Nuns are big on teaching me how to knit, patch holes and tears in clothing, and resole leather shoes. They also believe I need training on "becoming an educated young lady," so they are also pushing proper manners, politeness, and social skills like using silverware properly. I still can use more help with the social stuff.

*   *   *

Lou Ellen

Just when my friend's future appeared cheerful and promising, dark and stealthy political clouds swiftly blew into the Polish countryside. The resulting violent storm left its mark on Katerina's life and millions of other people for many years to come.

Invasion and Occupation

Lou Ellen

For the inhabitants of Horodenka and surrounding villages, September 1, 1939 began as a routine day. The sun was warm and bright. Cotton ball clouds dabbed the expansive sky, and owners of their clip-clopping horses brought carts full of squash, pumpkins, and other fall produce to the market square. Merchants readied their wares for customers at the meat market, leather goods and shoe stores, the tobacco shop, haberdashery, bakery, and apothecary, among others.

In the beginning, only folks who were outdoors heard a strange rumble in the distance. A novice nun weeding in the convent garden heard a strange distant noise. "What is that strange sound?" she asked a sister who was working alongside her.

"I don't know," the nun answered. "But we better hurry inside and tell the others."

Within the hour, Katerina remembered, the German military attacked Poland from the west, south, and north, marking the beginning of World War II. Five weeks following the invasion, Germany completely occupied Poland.

Katerina

Oh, do I ever remember the invasion, and especially the occupation? It is as clear in my mind now as if it was happening yesterday. In the beginning days of occupation, we peek from the convent windows off and on all day, watching the soldiers strutting around

35

like roosters and sashaying down the streets, choosing which houses to enter. Troopers either give the doors a few raps or kick them open and bust inside, regardless if anyone comes to the door or not. The sisters tell us the soldiers then rummage through every room keeping a lookout for a family's prized possessions or anything else of value they can get their measly hands on. Once outdoors, they whoop and holler and show each other their new treasures. In addition, when a family has a flock of chickens, I watch this myself, as soldiers put down their loot, go inside the pen, grab a chicken or rooster, wring its neck and head off, then, laugh and joke with their comrades. I do not forget one young soldier who stashes stolen goods under one arm and with his other hand grabs hold of his bloody, headless chicken by the legs and proudly marches away.

At first, the German soldiers wander around in front of the high cement wall that surrounds the convent, but so far, they do not bother us. We can even walk around the town center without having any trouble, that is, if a nun wearing her habit comes with us. Other sisters believe we have nothing to worry about, but most of us are scared. Every morning and at bedtime, Mother Superior checks all the doors and makes sure they are secure.

In a short time, though, everything gets worse. Many different shops and some banks close. Then food and money is hard to come by. Jewish families who manage to pull it off leave Horodenka, the place they have lived most of their lives. How sad. I will say this. What we do not see from our window, the nuns are good at keeping us older kids posted. Sister Mary says the Germans are now going after anyone who is Jewish. She also learns that the soldiers first target their homes and shops. If they discover a menorah in a home, the thieves snatch the family's valuables and return later for more loot. "When troopers leave the first time around," a sister explains, "they mark the homeowner's wall with a large black Jewish star or scrawl the word *Jew* all over the shopkeepers' front windows. The second time around, soldiers grab more booty and haul it out into the street."

The first time I witness this astonishing madness, I feel as if a runaway horse suddenly stops, rears up, knocks me down, and stomps. Still, I can't move away from the window.

Later, the Nazis force-march these poor Jewish mothers, fathers, and their children to the other part of town while they are prodding slow walkers with rifle barrels, trying to speed them up. Older men shuffle along with heads down. As I keep watching, men and troopers gradually fade in the distance and disappear. Even now, I still see people's faces stricken with terror. If anyone screams or yells, a trooper shoots him on the spot. I see this with my own eyes. Not many of Hitler's goons put up with screaming. For instance, when the locals walk outdoors and are minding their business, sudden screaming, yelling, or a loud disturbance will cause them to take off running and search for a less dangerous place. Rarely do you see more than two or three citizens chatting together in the streets. Germans will not allow large gatherings; if they come across more than three people together, soldiers quickly move in with carbines and warn people to move on or face death.

Before the occupation, it is usual for many friends and neighbors to gather in the streets where they chat about the weather, exchange family news or exchange political views. Now it is illegal for more than three or four persons coming together in public. Meeting in private is another matter. At least they will not be led away or shot; that is, if nobody finds out. I think the German invaders believe large citizen groups are up to no good, or worse yet, hatching a revolt.

By now, Jewish families do not even try leaving Horodenka. SS troops patrol the cobblestone streets on foot or horseback twenty-four hours a day—even on the main dirt roads that lead to other villages. We are stuck here, Jews, Poles, and everyone else, under Hitler's thumb.

Lou Ellen

For the most part, the Nazi reign of terror continued, but their entrapment methods changed. One incident, witnessed by several Horodenka citizens and made known to Mother Superior, the Sisters of Nazareth, and a few teens—including Katerina, was extremely disturbing. For days, that frightful news caused wholesale agitation and nonstop conversations within the cloister walls.

According to several witnesses, early rising neighbors in one area of town spotted a tank sitting in the middle of the street. It appeared abandoned. Not a soul was in sight. There was no tank crew nor anyone else guarding the machine. Neighbors figured it was either broken down or out of gas. All morning long, the vehicle sat, apparently abandoned. German soldiers and officers had disappeared. However, just as the town clock struck 12:00 p.m., a frisky boy with dark hair and skin tanned like a chestnut, emerged from a clump of trees and began checking out the tank. Suddenly, the top hatch opened, and two armed tankers jumped out; they screamed and shouted. The terrified lad ran for his life without looking back. Immediately, both soldiers shouldered their carbines. One man lowered his gun; the other aimed and fired repeatedly until the youth's lean body stopped jerking on the ground.

As the horrible incident was being described, Katerina said she heard the nuns commiserating among themselves, with a sister saying, "He was only eight or nine years old. What a shame."

"Well," an older sister moaned in resignation, "there goes another young innocent victim. How many more will they eliminate?"

Sister Mary Elizabeth let out a long sigh, shook her head, and blurted, "Dear God. What is this world coming to? When will it ever stop?"

*　　*　　*

Lou Ellen

On September 17, 1939, two and a half weeks after the Germans invaded and conquered Horodenka and other parts of Poland, Soviet forces invaded the country. In due time, the Red Army attacked and took over Poland's eastern section, while the Nazis occupied the western half. That portion now became a new German territory. Meanwhile, the Soviets were integrating the eastern half of Poland within the nearby Russian border. The USSR government declared that all Poles living in that area were new Soviet citizens.

For most Poles, the Red Army invasion and occupation of their country was very confusing. They could not imagine that a Russian takeover was even possible. Nevertheless, many believed Soviet propaganda, which claimed that their invasion would liberate the country from the Germans.

Katerina

Life is just as bad or worse now that the Russians are invading us too. At night, it is especially dangerous when Red soldiers prowl around for sex. They march from house to house looking for girls and young women. If parents with daughters argue or fight against the men, they do not have a hope or a prayer. Right away, the family is shot, and their heads are stuck on a fence post for every passerby to see.

Lou Ellen

During that period, Katerina remembered that Horodenka locals wondered whether the Russian army had a wager going with the Third Reich, which would determine which invasion force could steal the most goods and valuables from Polish citizens. It was common knowledge that the Red Army was poorly equipped and very hungry. The soldiers soon learned that most Polish homemakers baked their own bread and kept plenty of flour on hand. Thus, more and more Soviet soldiers stormed into people's homes and stole half their flour. In addition, the men raided smokehouses and robbed their contents: whole hams, bacon, pork hocks, and sausages, among other meats. As the soldiers left, they accused homeowners of possessing too much food. Oftentimes, they warned occupants, "If we decide to come back again, and you have all this food on hand, we will take it. Then you will have nothing." Under those circumstances, residents learned cleverness. In a short time, they were skilled at hiding small amounts of provisions they trusted were safe from discovery.

*   *   *

Public Domain Map of the 1939 Demarcation Line
Of Poland between Soviet Union and Germany

Katerina

A Russian soldier follows when I walk to my job at the hospital, but he doesn't bother me. It is here that I learn all the scuttlebutt about the Russian's evildoings and brutal acts. I listen to two nurses on the floor discussing what a friend says is happening at the asylum across town. She says the Soviet Union's secret police force comes to the mental hospital, grabs sick patients, whisks them away, and murders them. One flighty young nurse, who talks with arms waving all around, describes asylum workers as "helpless as fish out of water." She adds, "If one person opens his mouth, that alone seals his fate."

Reds also take over Polish businesses and factories. They close and destroy churches and religious structures. Polish banks are closed, and people's money disappears. Soviet forces capture more than two hundred thousand Polish soldiers as prisoners of war; many will probably end up and die in frigid Siberia and other distant sections of the USSR.

By now, I am sick with worry. None of the sisters or people in town can tell me where Father and Phillip are. Both are serving the fatherland, and I am afraid they are now prisoners. I only hope and pray they will survive and make it back home someday. What about Michalina? I do not and I will not ask.

*   *   *

Lou Ellen

In 1941, the Germans attacked areas of Poland that Russia previously annexed, and shortly thereafter, the troops captured the frontier posts. That act broke the nonaggression agreement the two countries agreed upon two years earlier. Therefore, when Hitler ordered his troops to invade the Soviet Union, Germany completely occupied Poland.

*   *   *

Katerina

Just when we think life can't get much worse, Hitler and his Third Reich goons return. They act like they are hell-bent on destroying our country, our people, and our culture. The Krauts take over farms, factories, and ranches. They close schools and lock church doors. Nazis ban prayer and worship. Defy these orders and you are a dead pigeon. For this reason, I do my praying silently inside my head. At the same time, teachers, professors, and priests throughout the land wind up disappearing. Storm troopers sweep into homes at night and take whole families away.

One day, a very tall middle-age officer comes to the convent's entrance. Mother Superior goes down to meet him. They exchange brief pleasantries, and then he adds that the gate to the ten-feet tall stone wall must be kept open during the daytime. She questions him, "Why? We never had to do this before."

He apologizes, says he is sorry, and explains that he is only following the orders of his superiors. "Please cooperate," he adds, "because if you refuse, I must order my tank crew to ram through it." The holy Mother backs down and explains that she will leave the gate open but will close and lock it at night for the protection of cloister residents. More discussion follows. "Now I must come inside with a few of my men," he says. Reverend Mother hesitates and then questions the reason for his request. "Just making certain some gutsy undesirable is not hiding someplace." Seconds later, he flashes a sheepish grin and adds in an I-am-sorry voice, "I am assuming without your knowledge, of course."

Suddenly, Mother Superior perks up. She breaks out in a sweet smile and pats the officer's hand gently. Her action puzzles me. What is going on here? Am I nuts, or is it my imagination?

Lou Ellen

At that moment, Katerina remembered that Mother Superior reached down into the folds of her habit and pulled out an envelope. She handed it to the officer. He quickly slid it in the breast pocket of his uniform. She hesitated for a moment and then said, "Okay, I will open the gate for you and no more than two of your men. First, you leave your machine guns and carbines in the hands of your soldiers while you search." The officer nodded consent, but he was not bubbling over with joy.

After Mother Superior unlocked the convent door, the officer walked from room to room, poked through storage areas, and checked out cubbyholes while two fellow soldiers watched with weapons at ready-to-shoot positions. The officer came up empty. "No traitors here," he announced. Upon leaving, the officer stepped aside with the reverend mother. Beaming like a burst of light, he patted his uniform jacket and thanked her for her time and inconvenience. "Oh, one other thing," he added, "my men and I make periodic searches, but do not become alarmed. It is merely routine."

*   *   *

Katerina

I remember Mother Superior as being old, maybe sixty or seventy years old. In fact, she is flat on top and husky below like a man—and by golly is she ever strict and tough. I don't think I will ever forget the three or four tiny curly whiskers that occasionally peek out from under her chin. In particular, her face is unforgettable. The deep lines on her cheeks, corners of her eyes, and under her nose and mouth still remind me of dry mud baking and cracking in the hot sun. In spite of her being a stickler for following rules and nitpicking at times, it takes a while before you know and understand her. In other words, when you constantly see Mother Superior treat her nuns and children with love, concern, and care, you view her as a true friend.

By the way, coming back to the incident between Reverend Mother and the officer, it seems apparent something is going on between them. Now when he makes his weekly visits, the two are all smiles and talkative. The officer treats Mother Superior with respect. She in turn appears to enjoy his company also. All the while, the two soldiers accompanying the officer stand down and relax. Meanwhile, with preliminaries out of the way, Mother Superior makes a sweeping motion, and the pair move to distant corner and continue their chat.

The entire time she smiles, laughs loudly, motions with her hands, and then quickly slips him a larger envelope. When I ask Sister Mary what could be inside, she chuckles and says, "Oh, just a little something to sweeten his day." Okay, I am thinking, if the two are on such good terms, why does Mother Superior have a nun go to the cupola in the daytime, when the gate is open, and watch the goings-on below. If the lookout spots anyone in a military uniform coming toward the convent, the crow whistle sounds. Instantly, young girls, novice sisters, and boys twelve years old and older, run for safety to the cellar. When this happens, a few handicapped youths, toddlers, elderly and ill nuns, along with resident maintenance workers, remain in the dining room area with the Reverend Mother. Able hands haul the table and the rug aside and whip open the trapdoor leading to the basement. Our hiding place is in the cellar one level below. A false wall covers the secret stairway. When we are settled below, the rug and furniture upstairs are put back in place, and everything looks normal.

No matter how many times we come down here, though, I am scared out of my mind. So is everyone else. My hands will not stop shaking. What happens if they catch us and take us away? Will they assault, torture, or kill us? Sisters try easing our anxiousness by murmuring, "Do not worry, boys and girls, keep praying. We will remain safe." Even so, I never forget one young girl, cute as a kitten, keeps twisting a piece of her blonde hair round and around her finger. In the corner sits a Jewish youth, whimpering. Sister pats him on the shoulder and follows with a button-your-lip sign. We sit on thorns and thistles for what seems like forever until we hear the all-clear clanging cowbell. Quickly, sisters blow out the flickering candles, and everybody climbs up the stairs and out of hiding. Thank God, I think. We are safe again. Will our luck run out next time?

Lou Ellen

Despite such terrorizing incidents, Katerina and convent youths who also had jobs at the hospital continued their work at the facility. It was located several blocks away from the convent. On one day, however, the teens headed to their jobs, skipping, laughing, and cracking jokes, when suddenly, she realizes that the hazy mist shrouds her group with heavy fog. At that moment, they had no clue that their lives, as well as those the world over, would change forever.

Based on the map made by the Service of Research and Documentation of the Ministry of Public Health and the Family (Brussels)

Capture

Katerina

The mist and thick pea soup takes us by surprise. We can barely see objects beyond our reaching arms and feeling hands. "Which way do we go?" someone whispers. "Right or left?" Everyone remains silent. No one knows the answer. Soon, confusion spreads like wildfire. Our hazy vision confuses our sense of direction. We have no choice except pray for God's guidance, ask Him for strength to plod forward, and, finally, plead for a good outcome.

Here in Horodenka, the shops and houses sit very close to sidewalks, so hand over hand, we feel our way along the sides of buildings. We take baby steps carefully until we reach an intersection. Somewhere in the mist, a loud booming voice, speaking German, shouts, "Halt! Halt! Do not move, swine. I can smell you already." We stop dead in our tracks. My heart pounds so hard and fast I feel it in my throat. At this point, not a soul knows what is happening, so one fellow in our group is brave enough to find out. Quick as lightning, with his voice cracking, he cries in Polish, "Everybody, stop right now, or these Germans will kill us."

Oh, dear God, I am thinking, *are you going to let us die?* Other kids who are somewhere behind me scream. Words stick in my throat. Suddenly, Nazis grab every one of us as if we are bothersome weeds and yank us along to a huge parked truck. They shove us up and push us inside. A huge canvas covers the back opening. Now we cannot see anything going on outside, and nobody on the street can see us sitting inside. As the truck rumbles on, some of us hold hands.

All of us are still and quiet like scared rabbits. We know the Germans hate commotion. If we do not cooperate or play dumb, there is no doubt that Hitler's soldiers will rap us alongside our heads with their rifle butts. Worse yet, they might even shoot us for fun. Finally, the truck stops. A trooper with a scary, angry look on his face whips the canvas open wide. "Raus! Raus!" he shouts. He motions with his rifle for all to get out and prods us along to a railroad car, sitting on the siding. We hang back and silently stand there like wide-eyed cows. Suddenly, the thought hits me. They will herd us inside that boxcar like cattle. A trooper slings his carbine over his shoulder and lugs open the large sliding door. Once we are up the ramp, he yanks us inside. There, we join a mass of other poor souls squashed together side by side like sardines in a tin. Many of them are sick and moaning. Others beg for "just a tiny bite of food' in exchange for "something valuable," and a few constantly cry out for water. The odor of urine, diarrhea, and vomit is overwhelming. Just when I think I will puke too, the door closes and locks.

*   *   *

Lou Ellen

It was Hitler's policy during this period to seize civilians from the streets of countries the Third Reich invades and utilize the continuous supply of workers as slave laborers in his war industry. Therefore, most of these forced workers, such as Katerina, are sent to thousands of concentration/labor camps existing in Germany and other occupied countries throughout Europe. Although most slave workers soon become half-starved or desperately ill, they are compelled to repair bombed railroads and bridges, work in munitions factories, industrial plants, and labor on farms. Refusal resulted in torture and death.

Katerina

We hear the rumble of oncoming trucks, brakes screeching, people crying, and soldiers who yell and blow earsplitting whistles without let up. We sit cramped on the wooden floor and breathe foul, stale air for what seems like hours on end. No one gives us food or water. Two boys sitting nearby whisper about their plan to make a hole in the floor by digging a knot out of a board. One teen says, "I have something in my sock. Hey, try this." He pulls out a large jackknife. Others offer what they have hidden inside their clothes: a letter opener, nail file, and a bent tablespoon.

Immediately, the young men take turns gouging, chipping, and boring into the stubborn knob. Off and on, they work all day long.

Hurray! Finally, we have a hole for air and a place to pee. I have been holding it until I think I will explode. Girls go first. Everybody agrees. One shaky voice asks the boys, "Will you shut your eyes first? Please." One by one, we pull down our pants, squat, and pee as fast as we can. Boys and men take their turns next. The floorboard hole is a busy place. Some folks stay where they are for different reasons: too weak or sick to stand up and move, already dying, or losing hope and giving up. Every day I remind myself that I will stay strong and make the best of a situation as long as I hope and pray.

Lou Ellen

Katerina and the other detainees fidgeted inside the dark odorous boxcar and worried about the outcome. She admitted that the uncertainty threatened to overwhelm her. She remembered her silent prayer.

Katerina

To this day, I remember most of it. It goes something like this: Hail Mary, God blesses you above all women because you are the mother of Jesus. Help us to stay alive. We are all lost souls here. We do not have the slightest idea where we are going or what will happen to us. Be with us always, amen.

I cannot help thinking about the nuns at the convent and those working at the hospital. When we don't show up for work or return to the convent after our shifts are over, everyone will wonder what has happened. Because they do not know, Mother Superior and the sisters will become sick with worry. I can hear them now saying, "What in the world do you suppose happened to them? Where are they? I think we need to pray for their safety, immediately."

Several times, I doze off and wake up to awful sounds: moans, whimpers, loud crying, coughing, and heavy breathing. "How long are we going to sit here?" someone groans. My dry mouth feels like sand. I do not know. Nobody knows. Forever, it seems. I lose track. Suddenly, there is shouting. The railcars creak and then rumble. Ah, we are finally moving at last.

The train makes a short stop at a station in Poland close to the German border. A nervous red-faced officer unlocks the with box-car and shoves it backward. For several minutes, the bright sunlight blinds us. "Stay," a soldier snarls, waving his rifle over us. "Halt," he barks. "*Verschieben sie nicht!*" (Do not move.) Quickly, he motions to a small man dressed in a white laboratory coat who stands beside him. "Come, Doctor. We are working against time here."

The doctor takes a quick glance at us inside, says we look okay but tells the officer to give us something to eat. A few soldiers hand out a single slice of bread spread with lard and one cup of water. Nothing else. Boy, does it ever taste good.

Lou Ellen

The train steamed ahead at full speed for several days. Eventually, it stopped at an area in Germany that resembled a military complex. A high metal fence topped with concertina wire surrounded the facility.

Katerina

A soldier in a gray uniform stomps back and forth in black leather boots in front of the open door. He motions for us to stand up and move out. At first, the bright sunlight blinds. Our lazy legs do not want to move. Older men and women take more time getting to their feet. They shuffle along slow and stiff. When another soldier pokes two old men with a club, they do not get up or say a word. For them, it is the end. The trip is over. For us, who knows?

I look around. Down the tracks are more railroad cars with men, women, and kids streaming slowly out. Gates open. Germans march us inside the compound and order us to "keep all eyes ahead and don't look left or right or ask questions." Just as if we are cows or sheep, they crack whips above our heads and scream, "Just go. Right now. Understand? Go!"

The Germans are like ants, crawling and scurrying everywhere over the grounds. A young woman asks, "Where are we?" A soldier tells her to shut up or "you'll get a bullet in your back." I do not speak German properly, but I do understand the meaning of most words. I have a knack for languages that way. I work with my brain until I figure it out.

In this place, there are rows and rows of barracks. In the middle is a large open field. The barrack in front of us looks nice and neat. Window boxes are filled with pretty red and white flowers. Barracks farther away look drab and beat up. Not a flower is in sight.

When everyone spills out from the railcars, orders are for us to form two long lines, one each for men and boys, women and children. Next, local farmers fan out, walk among the columns, and pick out healthy and strong-looking people for working their farms. "You, ah, no not you, but you over there," the farmers shout. They keep moving up and down the lines many times, deciding who to choose. So far, I am lucky. I do not get a second look from them, and they keep passing by. I feel safe until a smelly farmer chooses me. I am puzzled. Why me? Is he blind? I am short and skinny and I look strong as a stick. His inspection stare gives me the creeps. Next, he scowls. I hope and pray he changes his mind and moves on. When he moves closer and motions for me to turn around, his dirty overalls and muddy boots reek of disgusting barnyard dung. He looks and smells like trouble, so I keep my eyes glued to the ground. Maybe I will spot a bug, an ant, or a beetle. Instead, there are faded green boots going around and around.

Seconds later, in a snarly voice, he bellows, "Kommen." Well, I guess this is it. I am out of luck. I have no choice but eat dirt and tag along.

Lou Ellen

The farmer housed Katerina in a small room located adjacent to the cow stalls. A single bed that creaked and slumped in the middle, and a washbasin stained with tiny ribbons of rust, were the only furnishings.

Katerina

I eat meals with the family, but they put me sitting by myself at a side table. After supper, my main chore is cleaning the dirt and weed clumps off their six kids' shoes. Only when I finish with this job or any others do the farmer and his wife allow me to go to bed.

When five o'clock in the morning rolls around, I am dressed, have already eaten breakfast (a bowl of porridge), and am ready for work. My first job is hauling out manure from the cowshed. Next, he has me pushing a heavy wheelbarrow filled with cow pies up a steep, narrow ramp. Then I am supposed to dump the nasty stuff into the horse-drawn cart he will later haul away. I never do this work before, and I no can do it now. I try again but still fall short. I have no strength. This is man's work. Well, the old fart turns beet red, screams and hollers and calls me a "good for nothing, lazy Polish pig."

Lou Ellen

The following day, the angry farmer demanded she try again, that time with the wheelbarrow half-full. All she could manage was pushing the load halfway up. Furious, he stomped off.

Katerina

I work for this man a week straight, and I still no can do the job he wants. After not speaking to me for a whole day, he finally says I have to leave and adds that a person will pick me up by car and transfer me to a new place. No more than fifteen to twenty minutes go by when two men come in a black car and climb out. The driver, who is wearing a green military uniform and a steel helmet with two lightning bolts painted on the side, grabs me and shoves me in the back seat as if I am a sack of potatoes. The man on the passenger side must be an officer. He is wearing a gray tunic. His cap is also gray that has braiding just above the visor. Above that is a spread-eagle insignia with a swastika below. They both shake hands with the farmer, and we roar off.

Where I am sitting, I no can see a thing. The rear view and side windows are covered with a black cloth and taped. I no can see the men up front, either. A metal divider separates us. The longer I ride, the more I am feeling cold and afraid. I imagine all sorts of terrible plots these Nazis are hatching up. For all I know, they be driving me off to a secluded spot in the forest, shoot me, and then cover me up with leaves and take off. Nobody in the whole world would even miss me. Here I am, almost seventeen years old. I wonder. Is this the end?

Lou Ellen

Hours later, the SS men stopped at a station for gas. The driver asked Katerina if she was all right. She said she sensed that his attitude toward her had mellowed. "Not right now," she answered. "I have to go to the toilet soon, or I'll…"

For a moment, he hesitated and then said, "The policy is that you must stay in the car, but if you cannot wait, the lieutenant will go with you. Be quick."

Katerina

At the Damen WC door, the officer follows behind. In German, I say, "Nein!" I motion for him to stand inside the entrance while I go into the stall, shut the door, and do my business. He does not understand. Instead, he opens the stall and stands, staring at me. I wonder, *Are you dumb or nuts? What are you thinking?* I wave him out and shut the door. What a relief.

Lou Ellen

Thereafter, the men deposited their passenger inside a holding camp in southwest Germany. Briefly, the officers signed papers in the camp office, and they hurried away.

Meanwhile, an elderly woman whose salt-and-pepper colored hair, which was partially covered with a faded red babushka, walked up to Katerina, who was sitting atop a large pink-speckled granite boulder placed near the office. "My child, why are you sitting here all alone?" Katerina looked up at the worn thinning fabric around the woman's head and explained that after the SS men dumped her there, they took off. She told the woman that she felt lost and did not know what to do next.

Katerina

I explain that I have no clean clothes. I am sweaty and feel dirty. She says, "Wait a second. Stay right where you are. I'll be back in a minute." Soon she brings back underwear, a skirt, blouse, and a sweater. The clothes feel soft and fresh-air clean. I ask her where I can wash up. "You come with me," she answers. "I am Marta. I come from Czechoslovakia. Now I know who you are. You are the one the farmer says did not work out, so he sends you back." Yeah, that is me, I tell her. I am Katerina.

Lou Ellen

The old woman, limping slightly, led the way to a building where a musty odor reached Katerina's nostrils. Marta's living quarters comprised two small rooms, one of which contained a scarred wooden table with two chairs, large-and-medium-size iron pots, a few dishes, utensils, a washbasin, and a wood-burning cookstove. Marta utilized the second room as a makeshift sleeping area, also sparsely furnished with a single cot, and an upside-down wooden potato crate. It served as a table. There was also a small chest and a white enameled chamber pot. She stowed it inside a wooden box, which was kept out of sight until she brought it out at bedtime. Until that time, the box served as a footstool.

Meanwhile, the Czech woman dragged out from under her cot a dull-looking galvanized washtub where a musty odor reached Katerina's nostrils. She hefted a large pot of steaming water from the stove and dumped it into the tub. Next, she added a second container of cold water and told Katerina to shed her clothing and hop in. She handed her a rag and a chunk of soap.

Katerina

I scrub from the tip of my toes to my forehead. Marta, who speaks just enough Czech for me to understand, will not let me wash my greasy hair. Next, I ask her if I can wash my dirty clothes. Again, she tells me no. I am disappointed, but I lie back and enjoy the warm soothing water. The longer I soak, the better my mood gets. I wish I can sit here forever.

Lou Ellen

Once Katerina climbed out of the tub, Marta explained why Katerina could not wash her hair or clothing. "If I use more water now," she said, "the SS guy in charge of the camp will go crazy. Everyone here is allowed no more than two buckets of water a day. I also have washing to do, so put your dirty clothes in this small tub, add some of your bathwater, and let everything soak. We will wash it all with clean water tomorrow—even your hair, but separately, of course."

Katerina

After dark, when Marta knows the SS man or the water police, as she calls him, goes home for the night, I wash my hair and both of our clothes. After rinsing everything, we hang the items on clotheslines she has looped around the stove. Early morning, when my stuff is dry, she tells me to fold everything, and pile it in the corner. Then she says, "If they come to take you away, Katerina, you tell them you have to pick up your clothes first. You hear?"

Lou Ellen

That evening, Marta informed Katerina that the camp official was assigning her sleeping quarters next to her. Katerina was pleased, she recalled, even though the room was small, barely larger than a horse stall. It was, however, completely absent of furnishings, except for a straw mattress and a shabby gray woolen blanket lying on top.

The following day, Marta assumed the role of Katerina's mother hen. She cackled advice, strutted around inside and out, and pecked away at the rules. Immediately, it was obvious to Katerina that her Czech friend enjoyed special privileges. She wondered why. Was Marta a Nazi sympathizer, or traitor? A spy?

Katerina

Gradually, as we get to know and trust each other, I discover that Marta is also a slave worker. She says she was kidnapped and dragged to this holding camp where she now translates for many foreign camp workers and the German office help. She is fluent in several languages, and she knows enough words in other tongues to get by. Without her help, the office staff is as helpless as fighter with one arm, and it is the main reason every official treats her halfway decent. It makes her life a bit easier than it is for most people here. As long as she does her job and keeps out of trouble, she can walk around camp without worrying about some brute shooting her in the back or starving her to death.

On the other hand, she and I, and nearly every person here, know it is stupid trusting anyone. Why not? Well, because life can—and probably will—turn deadly in a second.

When Marta gets the chance, usually in the evening, she gives me lessons in what she describes as "important German words and phrases for you to learn that might save your skin later on." In other words, I am learning to stay in line and crawl on my belly.

I don't exactly know how long I will be here, but I am having a good time learning the language and being with Marta. She knows how to make learning fun and easy by playing little word games with me.

It bothers me, though, because I wake up in the middle of the night crying my head off, then I have trouble falling asleep again. The next morning, I wake up feeling sad and afraid; it happens to me at least two times a week. I have been here at almost one month, and I cannot figure out why I bawl like a baby. Nobody is beating me or threatening me, but I am unsure about everything. Right now, I have no control over my life, and this keeps me on edge. Marta constantly reminds me that I must keep my eyes and ears open always, and if I sense trouble nearby, I must move away as far as possible. I know. When storm troopers or the police yell at someone, and a friend butts in, he or she is just asking for a severe beating or worse. Most times, it doesn't pay to be a Good Samaritan.

Lou Ellen

Subsequently, a SS trooper squad stormed the camp and forced all its occupants to line up in rows on a football-size field. From the columns, a young officer selected healthy-appearing men, women, and children. In a hoarse voice, he said, "From now on, you will be working for our führer and the Third Reich, so prepare yourselves."

Katerina was among the group of one hundred persons selected. When she stepped out of line, waves of apprehension swept over her as she contemplated her future destiny and the fate of the many rejected people left behind. Immediately, she said the Germans marched the designated workers to an open field and herded everyone into the two-and-a-half-ton cargo trucks with tarp covers.

Katerina

As the truck I am riding in takes off, nobody dares ask our guard where we are going. Everybody knows better. Except for a few coughs, sniffles, and murmurs, there is no talking. We sit cramped and uncomfortable, with our knees and shoulders touching. For what seems like hours, we listen to whining tires, ride out the bumps and jerks, and breathe engine exhaust.

I shut my eyes and say another prayer just as the truck pulls up to the train station. Everyone climbs out. Soldiers shove us onto the train. The last thing I remember before falling asleep is swaying from side to side hearing the click-clacking wheels along the track.

Lou Ellen

Little did anyone know that the destination was a camp located in upper Bavaria on the site of a former munitions factory. The facility and its operation by the SS would later earn worldwide disgrace for cruel and murderous deeds. For example, illnesses of compulsory workers were ignored, as was various diseases and starvation. Furthermore, many a slave worker who lost all hope and could no longer tolerate his plight committed suicide.

Dachau Concentration/ Labor Camp

Lou Ellen

The concentration camp first opened in 1933 and was located outside the southern Bavarian town of Dachau. Munich was approximately ten miles away. Dachau was one of the first facilities in the Third Reich's expansive network of concentration and forced labor camps throughout Germany as well as conquered European countries. It was also the first such facility to utilize SS soldiers as guards. In the beginning, the camp incarcerated political prisoners such as communists, religious dissidents, gypsies, homosexuals, resistance fighters, and other undesirables Hitler considered were enemies of the state.

By 1941, the Nazi regime occupied more and more countries, and the Axis's need for slave labor increased. Not only did the Third Reich and its war machine benefit from those workers, many German corporations also profited from the practice. Companies such as Krupp, IG Farben, and Siemens purchased workers from camp administrators and ended up paying those men and women meager wages or none.

*   *   *

When the train stopped at a wooden platform outside the small town of Dachau, eighteen-year-old Katerina and her fellow internees disembarked. They looked around. Nothing was there except an expansive area of scrub land and weeds. Suddenly, an SS trooper shouted, ordering everyone to march. Two miles later, the weary stragglers shuffled through Dachau's iron entrance gate.

Katerina

Even today, I picture the heavy iron gate with the words *Arbeit Macht Frei*, which means work will set you free. At the time, I am thinking, what a big fat lie. Free? In the convent, I am free. Here, I am prisoner.

An older man in our group, a Pole, whispers, "Here we will die." I ask why, what does he know? "Because Poland fights against Germans," he says. "Now they will kill every one of us. Even Hitler's hatchet man, Heinrich Himmler, admits that all Poles will disappear from the world when the Germans destroy every one of them." Well, I pass his words on to the other men and women; first in Polish, German, and then in not-so-good Czech.

"All of you are so stupid," a young man who acts full of himself blurts out. "Nobody dies here. They need us to work. Do not believe a word she or anybody else says. This is a downright lie."

Well, guess what. Several months pass when I hear a story about this same cocky acting fellow. He leaves Dachau and winds up slaving away in a coalmine at one of Hitler's sub camps. The British begin bombing the camp for several days in a row. During the first bomb raid, he and two workers digging coal alongside him die. Strange, isn't it?

Lou Ellen

The Dachau camp, utilized as a training center for SS guards, was divided into two sections: the entire camp area and crematorium. The latter was located outside the prisoner camp. It contained gas chambers for delousing infested clothing, and the crematorium for incinerating the dead. In addition, seventeen barracks were located on both sides of the camp road, totaling thirty-two buildings. The complex also had a group of support buildings containing a kitchen, laundry, and showers. A courtyard separated the barracks from the prisoner camp where punishment such as pole hanging, whippings, and executions took place. In addition, an electric barbed-wire fence, a steep ditch filled with water, and a high-wall including seven guard towers surrounded the entire complex. Such deterrents discouraged most escapees, except the foolhardy or those in despair.

After the new arrivals completed a lengthy session filling out forms and other paperwork for the camp office staff, detainees listened to the camp administrator who cited rules, regulations, and examples of punishment one could expect for disobedience and non-cooperation. Only when such administrative duties were completed did the workers receive their barrack assignments.

Katerina's barrack, identical to the others, accommodated two hundred other women, all of whom were forced workers. Other barracks, also called blocks, housed political prisoners, dissidents, undesirables, male forced workers, and other groups Hitler considered his enemy. The blocks were divided into two sections, each with an outside door that opened into a small hallway. One door led to a room lined with toilets while the other entrance led to the washbasins.

In addition, each side of the main entryway included sparsely furnished living rooms and dormitories built to accommodate fifty persons each. The living area, Katerina noted, included wooden lockers lining the walls and several tables and stools for eating meals. The dormitory contained long three-tiers of crude wooden bunks. Loose straw served as mattresses, and makeshift blankets were thin and tattered.

The administration building, located at the east end of the complex, contained a small kitchen, a laundry, and storage rooms. Behind that structure was the camp prison where punishments and executions took place in the yard. Far from the living areas, on the outer edge of the camp, was a crematorium, designated as Barrack X. Adjacent was the gas chamber. It resembled a shower room with spray nozzles attached to the ceiling. When leery slave workers questioned its purpose, camp officials claimed its use was for debugging lice and other critters from incoming detainees' clothing and belongings. It was a preventive measure used to stave off typhoid fever, they said.

Katerina

I am a prisoner in this place, like my barrack mates. We do nothing but work. During the rare instances we are allowed free time, we spend it searching and picking nits and lice from each other's hair. The food we receive is just food to keep a bird alive, and my body begs for a decent night's sleep. The camp police, the SS guards, and their rules keep me constantly on edge: touch the fence, and you fry; step on the grass close to the ditch, and your head is the rifleman's bulls-eye; try to escape and…. It goes on and on.

All the women in my barrack work at different jobs in the parachute factory. I work the night shift starting at 6:00 p.m. The SS men march us to the factory, which is at least a mile or so from the camp. It is a good-size building, which is deep in the woods. If a woman cannot keep up with the other marchers or is so weak that she falls down, a trooper pulls out his pistol and shoots her in the head. I see this with my own eyes. Moving along, I have enough sense to keep my head down and look around out the corners of my eyes. The area looks like farmland, but there are no houses that I can see, no animals, and no workers around. I believe that Hitler's men give families a choice—leave or die. Hitler takes anything he wants.

In the factory, workers try out before the floor boss assigns them to certain machines or jobs. First, he demonstrates how the machines work. Then he harps on the importance of obeying safety rules. "We need you to work," he says, "not to get hurt." If he no likes a woman's looks, or if she fails his trial test, she's sent away to another area.

In my case, I am standing with three other women at the thread-making area where I watch each woman try out one of two crushing machines. He sends them all away. At the same time, he throws up his hands, makes a face, and wags his finger. I still don't understand why he picks me. I do nothing different from the other women, but I am much younger. They must be between thirty and fifty. It is hard to tell. Maybe I remind the boss of his sister or his girlfriend. On the other hand, it's possible he is interested in me. I hope not.

*　　*　　*

Lou Ellen

Hemp, which grew from six to eight feet high, was trucked to the plant and hauled inside. Bunches of the weed were then soaked in a pool of water. Following the soaking period, bundles were loaded into a large wood-fired dryer. When the dried hemp arrived at Katerina's station, she spread the material on a machine that crushed the outside layers. Thread-like fibers remained. Other work stations then processed the material, which eventually became parachute lines.

*   *   *

Katerina

After I am on the job a month, there is a huge blowup between a husky blonde farmer woman and the boss. Well, one day at her workstation, she grabs armloads of hemp and dumps it all onto the crushing equipment. Suddenly, the machine shudders, makes a loud clunking noise, and then freezes up. Now the boss comes running over to see what the problem is and if he can fix it. Foul-ups are good for operators because it gives us a short rest for a few minutes, and sometimes longer. Well, the boss starts swearing and calling this tough woman all kinds of nasty names and blames her for the breakdown. She comes back at him with, "I work with a threshing machine all my life, and I always feed it large bundles of wheat without any problem at all. Do you want to know the problem? I will tell you. Your machine here is nothing but a cheap piece of crap. You need to spend a few more deutsch marks and come up with a better one." Right away, we workers hold our breath, afraid of what will happen next. In a flash, he grabs her long hair, drags her away from the machine, and marches her over to the hemp soaking area near-by—a big hole dug into the clay floor that contains water. Anyway, he shoves her in. The water is up to her knees. She starts spitting, swearing, and splashing with her feet. Her shoes and trousers are soaking wet. "You ugly swine bitch," the boss yells at the top of his voice. "Get out of my sight and go work in another area."

The farm woman answers by spitting out streams of filthy talk and cuss words.

Lou Ellen

Once she caught her breath, my friend continued, the woman questioned his honesty, fairness, compassion, and the sense of justice. Katerina said she spoke to her in Polish and warned her to "shut up, or you will die." Nevertheless, the defiant woman stared hard at Katerina and then had the audacity to say, "Excuse me, Miss Nosey. This is none of your business, so why don't you shut the hell up."

Katerina

Another German dressed in a uniform—I don't know whether he is a camp police officer, an SS trooper, or some sort of guard—comes over to see what is causing all the commotion. She is still yelling at the top of her lungs and swearing a blue streak. The German hits her so hard with the butt of his rifle, she falls face down in the water. Nobody moves. I say nothing. I do not want to get hurt. I peek at the other onlookers. Sympathy fades from their faces. All eyes look down. All lips lock against sound. Everyone goes back to her job. Before long, two husky German soldiers show up. One guy pulls the woman's hair back, which lifts her face up and out of the dirty water. He hesitates then shrugs his shoulders. Each man grabs a limp arm and drags her away.

* * *

Lou Ellen

At six o'clock in the morning, the day shift arrived at the factory, so Katerina and her fellow workers trudged back to their block for breakfast. Without fail, it consisted of a half-cup of see-through lukewarm coffee and a slice of heavy wet bread. As the group neared the compound, they sniffed a distinctive odor coming from the tall brick smokestack spewing mouse-color smoke into the morning sky. Everyone turned dead silent. The stench triggered Katerina's memory of her childhood days in Horodenka, she said, when her father killed and dressed a chicken for supper. First, he pulled off feathers and removed the lantern's glass chimney. Then he held the bird over the flame and singed off its pinfeathers, leaving charred dots over its entire body. She recalled the tender feelings touching her heart, but from then on, her memory trailed off. The appetizing baked chicken odor, the succulent white meat, and a full stomach became a dim remembrance. However, she said the odor, the sympathy, and the tender feelings remained fresh in her mind.

Katerina

No matter how horrible, shocking, or crazy this place gets, you must eat. When I first come here, I do not eat for three or four days. I am so weak I can hardly walk. This makes me afraid the Nazis will wait until I die, feed me into the fire, and dance with joy that this Polish pig comes back to earth as black smoke and gray ash. I will not let this happen, so I eat their slop.

For lunch, our meal is one thick slice of bread. It comes so soggy and heavy it falls in chunks when I pick it up. Along with the bread is somebody's idea of chicken soup. Actually, it is yellow; warm water and a few mysterious green and orange flakes floating on top.

After everyone in the barrack finishes eating, we sweep, tidy up around the building, and sleep for a couple of hours. Waking up, we have supper before it comes time to begin the night shift. Supper is exactly the same meal as lunch, and the reason I am skin and bones—just like everyone else. While I am held captive here, though, I sometimes hope the Allied forces will drop a few bombs nearby to scare the Germans but not so close the whole place is blown to smithereens, and all of us are killed. Air raids are unpredictable, but when they do happen, sirens wail, factory work stops, and everyone runs outdoors hoping for safety in a nearby fenced field. In a way, most workers look forward to the raids. Not only do they give us a break from work, there is a slim possibility we will find something on the ground to eat which will calm our empty bellies. But then, nothing makes sense. Hitler forces us to keep his war machine going but starves us to death. Doesn't he realize that a well-fed healthy worker is more productive? I cannot tell you how many middle-age women workers I watch become weak, then sicken from lack of food, and wind up dying. You see the poor suffering souls in the morning, and the next day, they disappear. It is a fact of life at Dachau.

*   *   *

Frau Meier, the German woman in charge of my barrack, is tall and has a medium build. She pulls her shiny black-and-gray hair away from her face and tethers it into a ponytail. It flops up and down as she hurries about, overseeing inside work as well as escorting injured or very ill females to the sick room. She informs all her charges that she is a widow with four adult children, and all four, she says proudly, are serving Hitler and the Third Reich. She describes herself as a civilian worker for the SS. Even though she works for the SS, she definitely does not share the SS heart or character. For example, many times, she says to us, "If I'm here, I will do all I can to keep everyone alive. While I have this job, I swear I will never beat, brutalize, or mistreat anyone. Maybe God will smile down from heaven and reward me by bringing my children back home safely. Oh, everyone needs to remember something. Always stay alert. If a guard, SS officer, or anyone else in a uniform speaks to you, just put your heads down and follow his orders."

When the frau comes to work in the morning, she sometimes brings us baked potatoes. She hides them under her clothes. On Christmas day, she brings a special surprise—a fruitcake she bakes herself. At first, I am thinking Christmas will be no different than any other day until the camp director gives us the day off from work. At first, I don't believe him. Then I am suspicious. Maybe they will do away with every single one of us. The more I think about it, the spookier I get. I calm down when I hear the frau talking to Nice Guy Gunter, our name for a halfway decent SS officer. Frau Meier admits she is giving her girls a fruitcake. "Why bother?" he says.

"I'll tell you why," she answers. "They deserve something special. For goodness sake. It is Christmas!"

Nice Guy ambles around the room, all the while gazing up, down, and around as if he is on an important inspection mission.

Frau Meier trails behind. Finally, Gunter stops, turns around facing her, and nods his head. "Go ahead," he says. As soon as he gives her the okay, a young, high and mighty officer who stands nearby and overhears everything rushes over to Gunter. *"Nein, nein,"* he growls, shaking his head and clenching his teeth. *"Nicht fur schmutig schweine."* (No, no, not for dirty pigs.) Before he opens his mouth again, Nice Guy Gunter jumps all over him. He reminds the big-headed know-it-all that he is in charge. "Can you get it through your thick head that I outrank you, mister?" he booms. "Piss off and mind your own business."

*　*　*

A short time later, Frau Meier brings the fruitcake into the back room where she sets it on a wooden bench and hurries to cut it in very small pieces. Then she leaves. We go crazy, singing softly, "Joy to the world, it's a merry Christmas day…and fruitcake, here we come; yum, yum, gimme some." The truth is my itty-bitty bite tastes so good and fresh I think I have a taste of heaven.

We know that Frau Meier is a good, kind, and thoughtful person, but she must be very, very careful. If the Nazis find out what she does to help us, they will kill her, for sure. She is always warning us to keep our lips locked and say nothing. "If you remember what I tell you," she says, "I will only report you for minor infractions. Do not forget, ever! When I order everyone to work faster (*Arbeit snell*) put your head down, do as I ask immediately, and do not worry."

*　*　*

Lou Ellen

Two incidents at Dachau that occurred within weeks of each other served to fix into the minds of all slave laborers and prisoners, not only the futility of escape, but the horrible consequence for not obeying their captors' commands. For instance, Katerina related that the first occurrence took place on a scorching hot August day. She noted that along with a few barrack mates, they were sweeping and cleaning the area outdoors when they spotted the lovely, young French worker leaving the compound with a middle-aged SS officer. The two drove away in his black Mercedes. Katerina said she, and probably every observer, wondered where she was going and for what reason. Subsequently, Katerina pushed the situation into the back of her mind as she had to catch a nap before suppertime; she needed rest before she performed her job at the parachute plant.

Katerina

Gossip spreads throughout Camp Dachau like warm honey. One story goes that the two are passionate lovers out for a joyride with fun and games. If this is true, I believe every person here is a little jealous. I am.

Hmm, early the next morning, as I and the other night shift workers reenter the compound, we catch sight of a crowd milling around the flagpole. Our guard orders us to keep moving along toward the barracks. I cannot help but realize something horrible is happening. Judging from the crowd's silence and their faces expressing pain and sympathy, I soon discover the reason. An SS trooper is poking the French girl with a leather whip as she hangs from the pole with her arms stretched above her head.

All day long, she hangs with every person in camp keeping an eye on her. Once or twice, I see a guard or soldier touch her lips with a wet sponge on a long stick; nobody gives her food. In other words, if the French beauty and her SS man are crazy in love, what goes terribly wrong and brings her to this situation? Again, several women give their opinions. The one view, which makes most sense, is this: At some point during their ride, the couple has a heated argument; it gets worse and turns into a knockdown drag out fight. Angry and exasperated, he jams on the brakes. She sees her opportunity and bolts out the car door. The officer jumps from the Mercedes, gives chase, and catches her. He hauls her back to the compound, indicates to authorities he is finished with her, and orders them to take care of her.

*   *   *

Meanwhile, the next morning as we night-shift workers are returning to the camp after working all night long, we enter the gate tired and gloomy. Suddenly, we realize the flagpole is bare. She is gone. On the one hand, I am heartbroken. On the other, I am glad. She no longer puts up with hunger and pain. As far as the true story goes, internees know better than ask authorities for more details. Experience makes us deaf, dumb, and blind—no matter what. If we let our emotions get the upper hand, we will pay for our foolishness later.

Even so, the sight of the French woman's white limp form dangling in the blazing sun with her head down and her awful moaning is one I will never erase. The memory of her pain and agony, even today, breaks my heart and brings on tears.

Lou Ellen

In the second event, failure to obey a directive or order, no matter how senseless, would usually result in severe beating, torture, or even death. At the time, my friend and her female barrack mates heard an SS soldier (patrolling outdoors) caution someone against gazing out the windows while he was on duty. Katerina and a few others hurried to a window nearby. There they saw a young woman who ignored his warning. She held her ground and said, "This is another example of your stupid, idiotic Nazi rules."

Katerina

She is such a nice, pretty girl. We practically beg her to stay away from the window, but she will not listen. She returns to the window and just stands there, calling his bluff. He rushes over, rests the gun barrel against the glass, and fires. At the rifle crack and sound of shattering glass, we move further away, crying and carrying on like babies. Blood flies all over. Before long, two camp workers come and drag her away.

The morning after, when the night shift ends at the factory, and we trudge back to the compound, the smoke and stench pouring from the brick chimney catches our attention, but I and the others pretend to ignore it. We keep walking. I cannot forget that poor girl hanging in agony, the farm woman face down in water, and the girl who will not move away from the window. Here I am, trying to forget their situations with little success. The horror of it all sticks to my mind like glue, and any reminder sickens me to the edge of throwing up. My stomach keeps churning. I feel it coming. I stop and bend over. The vomit erupts violently. The urge to puke returns again and again. A few dry heaves, and it is over.

*   *   *

Lou Ellen

Captives were forbidden to talk among themselves almost everywhere, except in their straw-covered bunks. However, a few women, including Katerina, seized the opportunity on Monday mornings when they were assigned outdoor duties such as sweeping with willow brooms, pulling weeds, or picking up small sticks and branches. Risk-takers were wary of being caught. Consequently, they devised clever tactics.

Katerina

Frau Meier usually divides us by two, tells us what the work is, and we do it. When the guards, who constantly walk up and down and around the compound, spot us talking or bunching up together, they believe we are up to no good. Then without a saying a word, they kick and punch anyone close by. Naturally, we learn a few little tricks. My favorite is sweeping dirt paths so quick and furious that billowing clouds of dirt and dust kick up. Almost every time, a guard will turn his back and hurry away just to keep his black leather boots clean and shiny. After he moves away, my partner and I do our soft hurry-up whisper.

The best time for conversation is on Sunday nights when there is no work at the factory and most women are lying in their bunks chatting or complaining to their friends and a few others they trust. Talking mostly stops after Frau Meijer turns off lights and locks the barrack door behind her.

Lou Ellen

In Dachau, as was the case with most concentration/labor camps throughout occupied European countries, near starvation, brutality, and demoralization among detainees were commonplace. Because of such intolerable conditions, millions of adults committed suicide. Many others died from other methods such as shootings, beatings, or hangings by guards and SS officers. Oftentimes, German officials falsified records of those violent deaths and attributed the causes as suicides.

During Katerina's second year of forced labor producing parachute thread for Hitler's war machine, she recalled the suicide of a young woman who lived in a nearby barrack.

Katerina

I never forget this woman. Her job assignment is at an ammunition factory near the village of Dachau. Some say she comes from a wealthy family. All I know is when she first comes to Dachau, she acts uppity, but she doesn't know her right foot from the left. I imagine she never lifts finger at home since the family cook and housekeeper handles these household chores. As it turns out, she just cannot bear her life and work here and doesn't have the patience or strength to make the best of it. So what does she do? She grabs a fistful of gunpowder at the factory and somehow gulps it down. A few hours after she comes back to the barrack one day, she falls down and dies a slow death. What a waste. I feel sorry for people like her who never know the meaning of work and cannot adjust to situations—they do not survive for long, especially in camps run by Nazis.

Other people collapse and die every day, many times on their way to the cafeteria for breakfast. When this happens, the SS push the dead off to the side, have workers lift them into wheelbarrows and dump their bodies outdoors onto a pile for final burning.

Even though many people here pass away day and night, the Germans keep bringing into camp new people of every nationality. Many are Polish, Russian, Yugoslavs, Italians, and even undesirable Germans.

Not a day goes by without the Nazis screaming at somebody or walloping the tar out of some timid soul. After viewing so much horror and brutality, I am learning that I must act like a zombie and block all the bad stuff out of my mind. If I do not do this, I am positive I will go crazy.

*   *   *

Lou Ellen

Under such circumstances, Katerina and her female workers were reluctant to report illness or minor injuries to factory bosses. Instead, many women struggled through injury, illness, and fear until labor became unbearable for them. Katerina recounted her first-hand experience regarding this matter.

Katerina

I am working at the thread station around ten o'clock in the evening. All day I am not feeling well but weak, achy, and a bit sick to my stomach. Around midnight, I go to the toilet. When I pull down on the flusher chain, I find bright red blood. This makes my hair stand on end. On the other hand, I wonder if I am having my menstrual period.

Lou Ellen

As is the case with so many other women forced to work in such camps, Katerina has not had a period in more than a year. Nonetheless, she hurried back to her station and informed the female supervisor of her plight. "Come," the supervisor said, gesturing. "You need to go to the treatment room. I will go along with you."

Katerina

At the infirmary, the German nurse at first stays tight-lipped then flares up in anger. Suddenly, with no warning whatsoever, the battle-ax smacks me across the face and calls me a lazy swine. "You don't fool me one bit," she snarls. "You're trying to get out of work, so you come here and pretend you are sick. Isn't this the truth?"

My boss, who is also a German native and takes her supervisory responsibilities seriously, is sincere and shows concern for us. "No, she is not lazy at all," she argues. Katerina is one of my best workers, but she is bleeding badly. Can't you see it running down her leg?"

The nurse snaps back. "What's the difference? She is one less sow our führer must deal with."

Lou Ellen

Shortly thereafter, Katerina complained of wooziness, dropped to her knees, and fainted. When she recovered, the nurse gave her a spoonful of bitter-tasting medicine and warned the supervisor not to bring Katerina to the treatment room again, or both would regret it.

Katerina

While we walk slowly back to work again, my boss feels bad and blames herself for not fetching the medicine herself and bringing it back to me. I thank her for everything she has done and praise her for showing me kindness. I really hope she receives her reward someday for doing what is right and proper. As I look back on the incident, the lesson I learn is that no matter how horrible and ugly a situation might be, there are always a few good individuals willing and able to help.

Lou Ellen

During the war years of 1942 and 1943, the British and Allied forces intensified bombing German targets such as railroads, harbors, industrial areas, and later, large cities. American pilots conducted daylight raids while the Royal Air Force bombed at night. Oftentimes, those pilots used the still-burning fires—from American daylight bombing—as navigational aids.

Allies believed that bombing cities gave them a psychological advantage by breaking the enemy's fighting spirit. Although that theory was debatable, dropping bombs on highly populated areas resulted in many civilian casualties and deaths.

Nighttime bombing raids in nearby towns and cities were frightening and becoming more frequent, noted Katerina. She cited one occasion while she was at work on the thread-making machine situated on the ground floor. Shortly after midnight, a sentry heard a distant droning sound. Word spread throughout the plant like spilled paint. Workers and machines came to a dead stop. Suddenly, an ear-splitting siren wailed, warning everyone of approaching aircraft. As she continued, she said that those bombing threats triggered mixed emotions among the women laborers. Some women tried to rein in their fears and anxieties against the risk of being maimed or killed. Others renewed their hopes for Hitler's defeat, the war's end, and the prospect of returning home. However, when the jarring alarm continued, hope and fear intensified for everyone.

Katerina

Personally, I pray to God that the planes will keep coming. Then the bosses will let all of us first-floor workers run outdoors. Those who work in the basement stay put. When the sentries watch the planes come closer, they fling open the gates. Quickly, German soldiers scramble and yell for all to evacuate. We beat it as fast as we can out into the nearby field. I find a small head of cabbage. Boy, do I ever eat fast, munching like a cow on limp yellow cabbage leaves with wormholes and all. Like the others, I then drop down on my knees and with my hands scouring the ground for anything else to stuff into my mouth. Those who find whole carrots and stubs gobble them down at once. No one cares when their finds are limp and dirty. Anything is good enough for an empty belly. I also find a few scrawny potatoes that I immediately hide in my overalls. At the same time, the planes apparently fly over the camp since we now hear bombs exploding in the distance on the horizon. Frau Meier explains that the British are night bombers while the Americans bomb during daylight.

Thank goodness, the airplanes disappear, and on this night, we are safe. Now that we are back inside and settling down, it is back to work. Before long, an officer in a brown uniform sashays around the plant, counting people. How dumb can he get? For crying out loud, nobody in her right mind is going to escape when a pilot might swoop down and spray everything in his path. Even so, this jackboot circles around the floor and says, "I do not want to hear one complaint that you women are stealing from the fields during air raids, or I will send bullets into your brains or beat you all to death. You get to choose which."

Well, at this point, I don't give a rip and doubt that many others care, either. We have to scrounge around for anything we can find and eat. All we think about is food and filling our bellies. We never get enough.

By daybreak, my shift is over, and I am back at the barrack, cooking potatoes. I bake them in the wood cookstove along with other women who are pulling their finds underneath their clothes. You see, Frau Meier always keeps a big pot of water on the flat stovetop with fire underneath that she always keeps going. When she goes home for the night, the frau chooses a few barrack mates she trusts to feed the fire until she returns in the morning. Anyway, I am just about ready to swallow another delicious bite of smoky dwarf-size potato when a soldier sneaks up behind me and scares me half to death. He asks what I have in my mouth. "A piece of almost-burnt tater I find on my way back from work," I say. "Why, I'll even share it with a handsome Jerry like you." My honey tongue and bright smile does the trick. He acts happy as a pup with two tails. *"Danke schon,"* (Thank you very much) he says, walking away. It never hurts to be nice. A little bit of flattery also helps.

Liberation

Lou Ellen

The year was 1943, and war raged throughout Europe; Hitler continued his quest for a pure, superior race. Dachau village people were celebrating a traditional German holiday with family and friends. The mood was festive. There was much music, dancing, drinking, and lively conversations. The merrymaking concluded with booming, brilliant fireworks. On the contrary, in Dachau's concentration/labor camp, daily life remained the same: starvation, illness, fear, depression, kicking, slapping, punching, and killing.

The following day at the labor camp, twenty-year-old Katerina and several other women noticed two strangers wandering around the compound. One of them was a clean-shaven man who appeared forty years old. Accompanying him was a middle-aged woman. She was dressed in white from her shoes to her cap; the center bore a small embroidered red cross.

Katerina

In broken Russian, I say to the few people I trust that we have some visitors. We better say a prayer because we don't know what will happen. Why are they here? The longer we try to come up with answers, the more nervous we get, so we sit on the dusty barrack floor in a little circle and hold hands. My friend, Helena, begins prayer. She starts like this: "Dear Father in heaven, please help us out of this awful misery because we don't think we can last this much longer. We know you are watching over us always, amen."

Right away, a nasty Ukrainian woman who admits she doesn't believe in God comes up to our little circle and says, "Huh, none you will survive, but I will. You will see." Nobody says a word, but I think to myself maybe she is right. Maybe she is wrong. Who knows?

Well, by the time Sunday rolls around, and a few of us are outdoors picking up twigs, yanking weeds from the flower beds, and sweeping here and there, we spot the same two strangers we notice earlier. The man and woman are watching our every move. Suddenly, he points and motions. I motion. Me? *"Kommen sie bitte hier,"* (Come here, please) he says. I think, *Oh my gosh*. The other girls are scared to death. Finally, I ask if I can help him.

Lou Ellen

The man suggested that Katerina turn around, giving him a closer look at her. "Once more, please," he added. He turned to his female companion and pointed out that Katerina was as skinny as a stick. Again, he faced Katerina and said, "All you need is a little more meat on your bones, but we can fix that later. Will you work for me?"

Katerina

At first, I hem and haw. I don't have enough information, so I ask, "Where will I go? What type of work do you need?" He says, "You will work for me in Berlin caring for our wounded soldiers. Incidentally, I am Dr. Josef, and this lady beside me is my nurse, Fraulein Tanya." His offer sounds good. After all, anything is better than this hellhole, so I accept. Then the doctor adds that he needs a second worker and invites me to select another person I know well, one who works hard, follows directions, and is friendly. Without hesitating, I choose my Czech pal, Helena.

I know and understand Helena better than anyone else at Dachau. She is my very best friend. Really, we are like two peas in a pod, and I know we will love working together. Even though she is older than I am, it seems like she depends on me for almost everything. Our bunks are close together, but since I work the night shift and she works days, the only chance we get to whisper a few words is when shifts change. Otherwise, we say things with our face and eyes.

Right off, I know how she is feeling from the look on her face: it is either sunny or dumpy. When she rolls her eyes, she finds something disgusting, or else she thinks an order or idea is stupid. Helena is a good, kind person, but she worries about everything, and it seems she is always afraid. She cries a lot too, which is very annoying at times.

Lou Ellen

Finally, Katerina called Helena over. She came timidly with her head down and her eyes glued to the dusty ground. Katerina related the details while the doctor and the nurse looked on. Whispering, Katerina then asked Helena for her opinion. In a voice, barely above a whisper, she said, "I can't wait to leave and go with you, but do you think he will do something bad like beating us to a pulp, or worse yet, violating us?"

Katerina

I take a stab at assuring her, saying, "No, sweetie, nothing bad will happen." Next, I advise her that she must truthfully answer any questions the doctor might ask. Still, she is wavering. Her voice quivers as she says, "Do you really think we are safe leaving here with complete strangers, or will we be sorry?"

"Stop being silly," I tell her. Of course, we are safe. It may be our only chance for leaving Dachau and staying alive. Besides, I know we are making the right decision. She still isn't sure. By now, I am losing patience with her. I beg her to quit her stupid worrying. I even threaten to end our friendship. Before she thinks this over, Dr. Josef interrupts, then asks Helena if she speaks German. When she tells him only a little, I suggest when he questions her, I will translate into Czech. When she answers him in her language, I will translate her words to him in German. Everyone agrees. Dr. Josef suggests I tell Helena that he will be pleased if she joins his medical team and assists with meeting foot soldiers' needs for rest, recuperation, and socialization. "How does this sound? Are you willing?" Taking me by surprise, Helena runs over to the doctor first, pumps his hand up and down several times, hustles over to the nurse who is standing by, and does the same. In her excitement, Helena babbles, "Oh my gosh. Thank you, sir. Thank you very much."

Dr. Josef smiles and goes on to say, "I trust that you two will appreciate the fact that I will pay the camp commander a hefty sum of money for properly signed documents, which give me permission to hire you. Then after you begin work for a short time, I will pay meager wages. However, when I believe your hours on the job equal the commander's price, I will pay you well. Do you have any questions? Well, if not, do you accept these terms?"

After I translate all his words to Helena, I nod my okay. She does the same, but now her tears start falling. In her stop-and-start voice, she says, "I don't care about the money right now. Just as... long as I...stay alive, I...don't care."

Lou Ellen

Subsequently, Katerina, Helena, Dr. Josef, and Fraulein Tanya walked over to the camp office. Upon entering, the camp commander, an SS officer, barked, "What are you people doing here?" Dr. Josef suggested that Katerina and Helena wait in the hall.

Katerina

Helena and I stand waiting in the hall just outside the commander's doorway. Surprisingly, we have no trouble hearing the conversation. First, Dr. Josef introduces himself and his nurse to the commander. Next, he does not waste words but makes it perfectly plain that he is "willing and able to pay a good price for these two young women." He goes on saying, "Both ladies will accompany us on our return to Berlin where we sorely need help."

Then Fraulein Tanya speaks up, saying, "We have so many sick and injured soldiers coming from the battlefront, we need to return soon as possible."

Helena and I have no trouble hearing the commander get up on his high horse. "Dr. Josef, sir! Fraulein! Do you forget I am Fredrick Schultz? As a senior lieutenant here, I make the rules, no one else. You bring somber news I regret hearing, but what gives you the idea you can bring these two dirty swine before my presence and inside my building?"

Helena and I are listening to everything going on in the office. Dr. Josef sounds like he is ready to explode. His voice gets louder and louder. He asks Schultz if he knows who he is talking to. "I am a surgeon—and a colonel, Lieutenant Schultz."

Schultz keeps nitpicking. He goes on, saying, "Ah, so, Colonel Josef. Are you threatening to pull rank on me, now?"

Dr. Josef makes plain that he will pull rank if he finds it necessary and adds, "You definitely can count on it, Schultz."

Schultz does not give up. He maintains he does not care who Dr. Josef is because as Dachau's commander, his are the only decisions that matter.

"I do not care who you are," Schultz argues. "I am the person in charge here, and what I say counts. That's it—end of discussion."

"All I want is two young ladies who know how to work," the doctor explains. "They must be young and healthy because they will be on their feet all day working fast and furious as they tend to our patients."

By the way. All us girls have a couple of secret, nicknames for Commander Schultz. One name is Rhine Monkey just because he has a fat, round belly. Another name is Fat Farty Fritz—my favorite. He is constantly breaking wind and making little putt-putt noises as he walks around. We think it is strange, but funny he is constantly gassy. Helena jokes that he craves sauerkraut so much he probably gobbles it down for breakfast, lunch, and supper.

Oh, well. Back to Schultz. After Dr. Josef explains that he needs good, healthy workers like Helena and me, the commander puts us down. "Huh," he says. "These two are no good. Look how sickly pale and thin they are. Mark my words, Dr. Josef. You are making a huge mistake. Most of these workers are sick and dying. Why bother spending money on them."

By this time, Dr. Josef has enough. He shouts, he bellows, "Listen, Schultz. I respect you as a commander, but frankly, you have a big mouth. My nurse and I do not make a trip here to listen to your garbage, but I come for good workers. I watch these young women working outdoors around the barrack sweeping, pulling weeds, and doing other chores. These are the two I want and will pay you for."

Lou Ellen

Schultz contended that all slave laborers were small nothings—specks of dirt on the road in the broad scheme of the Third Reich. Dr. Josef countered with "That is your opinion, Schultz, not mine. The two young women will work out just fine."

Quickly, Josef pulled papers from his pocket, proving to Commander Schultz that he was authorized to take the young women from Dachau. Schultz scanned the documents carefully, shrugged, and then noted that everything looked in order.

Katerina

After Dr. Josef pays for Helena and me, he and Nurse Tanya come out in the hall where we are still waiting, and now wondering if we are dreaming. Neither one of us can believe our turn of luck. Next, Dr. Josef orders the commander to outfit us in clothing. Down the hall, Schultz enters a storeroom and hauls out a huge armload of shirts, socks, gloves, caps, pajama bottoms, underwear, and trousers—all stuff for men.

Lou Ellen

Impatient and angry, the doctor lost his temper. "Dammit, Schultz," he snapped. "You are either a fool or stupid. Are you blind? These young women cannot wear men's clothing. What is wrong with you?" Stammering, Commander Schultz dug deeper into the closet and eventually yanked out shirtwaists, skirts, dresses, and several clean-looking but well-worn underwear. After the clothing was gathered, Fraulein Tanya suggested that the two young women return to their barrack, wash themselves, and then change into the clean garb.

*   *   *

Inside their barrack, Katerina and Helena were anxious to tell bunkmates their good fortunes. Upon hearing the news, many of them were happy for the pair and wished them well. However, several other women were mean and nasty.

Katerina

In no time at all, these four women who have their own tight circle come together and right away start whispering. One accuses me of "kissing some German's hind end for a ticket out of Dachau." Another jerk, a hoity-toity blondie who thinks she is hot stuff, calls me a whore. Then the Czech witch, who brags she doesn't believe in God, accuses Helena and me of sleeping with SS officers and doing other repulsive things. We hear these awful lies the whole time we are gathering our few belongings. One member of the circle does not say much, but jealousy and disapproval spread over her face. This kind of nastiness burns me up and hurts at the same time. Helena is hurting too, but I practically beg her to let it all go. People who do these kinds of things are bitter; they have no hope, and they probably will not survive this ordeal.

Before long, our barrack supervisor Frau Meier brings soap and buckets of warm water for quick baths. After pulling off coveralls and underwear, we scrub our heads and bodies. Oh, it feels wonderful when I scrub away my body odor and finally stuff my dirty smelly work clothes under my bunk. We dry off and put on underwear and plain cotton dresses Schultz hauls out from storage. Helena's outfit is at least twice as large as she is. My dress touches the floor, and I am constantly stepping on it. Even so, we could care less so long as we leave this place.

Helena grins from ear to ear. "Wow, Kate," as she calls me, "doesn't it feel great wearing dresses for a change?" I agree with her but notice her happy face is fading away. I remind her that soon we will climb into Dr. Josef's car and go off to a better place. We will survive, I stress; if we stay here, we will not.

Taking me by surprise, Helena puckers up and sobs. "You always say this, Kate, but I don't believe you. I know something will go wrong, and I will die here."

For crying out loud, I do not understand her, and without thinking, I give her a piece of my mind. For heaven's sake, I say, "What in the world is wrong with you? You should be happy. We are getting out of this hellhole, and you are worrying about all the bad things that could happen. If you don't change your attitude, I doubt if you will make it. Start looking on the bright side of life. Stop depending on me and other folks so much and grow up. You will feel better about yourself and other people. You realize, don't you, that once we leave Dachau, we will at least have a chance at life? It will not happen here. Use your brain."

Now I am so angry with Helena, I have mixed feelings. Should I lecture her more or called it quits? Before I decide, Frau Meier returns and offers to walk along with us to the office, which is a kind gesture. Then just before we leave the building with Dr. Josef and Nurse Tanya, Helena and I thank Frau Meier for everything she has done for us—watching our backs, sneaking food for us, and keeping us alive. We hug and cry while our two rescuers patiently stand by. Soon Frau Meier's tears turn into rivers streaming down her cheeks. She is such a good, loving German woman, I hope and pray that her children will survive the war and return home with no injuries to their bodies or minds.

Lou Ellen

After everyone walked toward Dr. Josef's car, he explained to Helena and Katerina that they would motor to the hospital in Berlin where he is temporarily assigned. "My wife Gerta," he added, "will give you both my grown daughter's clothing. I do not know what we will do with this one, (Helena) though. She is so small, we may need to buy her something to wear. We will see. My wife is used to these things, and she is a very good seamstress."

Along the way, Katerina related, Helena grabbed onto her hand and hung on for dear life. She compared Helena's clinging to the pesky head lice and nits that camp women constantly picked and combed out of the hairs on their heads.

Katerina

As we are speeding along on the autobahn, it is such a relief knowing that Dachau is finally and thankfully an experience of the past. Straightaway, Dr. Josef explains that Berlin is 493 kilometers away, which means two driving days with an overnight stay at a hotel. He urges me and Helena to relax and enjoy the ride in his nice blue Mercedes sedan. He also encourages us to take long restful naps—if we feel like it.

Lou Ellen

On day two of the trip, Dr. Josef accepted Nurse Tanya's offer to drive the remaining 246 kilometers (153 miles). He cautioned her to be vigilant for low-flying aircraft. Further, he announced he was "going to rest his eyes a bit." At the same time, the two young women sitting in the back seat resigned themselves to a three-hour tiring, boring ride. Both finished browsing through many German-language newspapers and magazines, and Katerina was weary from answering questions and translating from the German language to Czech for her friend. Suddenly, a nerve-shattering situation occurred, and boredom erupted into panic and fear.

Katerina

We are cruising along with Fraulein Tanya at the wheel when she unexpectedly slows down and shouts, "Wake up, Doctor! Look quickly to the right. That plane is coming toward us low and fast." Dr. Josef jerks upright as Nurse Tanya slams on the brake. He yells for everyone to get out and run. There are many trees along the roadway, but he points to what looks like a one-hundred-year-old oak and shouts, "Go to that one. Hurry, hurry." Well, the trunk on this tree is so huge the four of us holding our shaky hands together cannot go around it. The ground underneath the overhanging branches and large green leaves gives off a strong earthy smell. As the plane's engine whines louder, I squeeze my eyes, closing them tight. I will not open them up. In my mind's eye, I picture this gigantic oak tree with its massive branches and leaves, sheltering us like a mammoth umbrella from bombs and debris. Playing it safe, though, I offer up a silent prayer, just as the plane skims low, pulls up, and disappears. Moments later, Dr. Josef's deep jumpy voice shouts a warning. "Look. He's coming back. Keep down and don't move."

Any second now, I brace myself for a thunderous blast that will probably blow us to smithereens, and I am terrified. I feel my heart bouncing and pounding against my chest. Suddenly, it enters my mind, *Please God, I do not want to die. I am too young and not ready yet.* Again, I squeeze my eyes, grit my teeth, and silently recite the Psalm 23. Suddenly, appearing out from the billowing clouds, the plane flies overhead and zooms by. Everyone stays crouched until the whining engine fades away. Shortly thereafter, Dr. Josef says in a cheery voice, "Wow. That was close, ladies. We can thank our guardian angel for that, don't you think?"

Berlin Krankenhaus

Lou Ellen

The hospital (*krankenhaus*) in Berlin was a massive red-brick structure whose buildings and grounds occupied nearly seventeen acres. Prior to 1941, the facility operated as a civilian general hospital until the German Reich purchased the entire plant. Thereafter, it became a hospital for the *Waffen-SS*. Its facilities in the main building on *heerstrasse* (street) were duplicated underground. Access to the hospital was through the sub-basement, by entering through massive four-feet thick blast doors.

Upon their arrival in Berlin, Katerina and Helena occupied temporary living quarters in a former storage room on the hospital's main floor. The following day, Dr. Josef instructed the pair to spend their first workday with Nurse Tanya for orientation. She would assign jobs and provide instructions. Further, the physician explained that he and his colleagues were providing care for German battle casualties coming back from fighting Russian soldiers on the eastern front. The staff also tended to medical needs of nonfighting Nazi party members, he added.

Katerina

Oh my gosh. The injuries I see the first day on the job are unbelievable. Why these young German soldiers, most look like boys, come in with missing hands, arms, and legs, now bloody stumps. Then there are the terrible gaping head and chest wounds. My job is to gently wash them, clean wounds, and apply clean dressings. I feed them and help get them into bed. I also take on all the other thankless and unpleasant chores the nurses dislike, including emptying bedpans, making beds, changing linens, and mopping floors. Helena is chicken-livered when it comes to hospital work. After her first week on the job, she decides she wants no part of nursing. She cries on my shoulder, saying, "Katerina, I just cannot stand to do this, dealing with all the blood, oozing puss, the blank stares, and frightened looks on young men's faces. I cannot take this any longer. It keeps me nervous and sick. If I have to stay here, I swear. I will kill myself first."

"Come on," I tell her. "This is only your first week. You will get used to it. Just give it a chance before you do or say anything." Does she take my advice? Heck, no. She pays no attention and wastes no time repeating her unhappiness to Dr. Josef.

A couple of weeks go by, and Helena is still stewing in her misery until the doctor hatches a plan with his factory manager friend. The friend will pay him the same amount of money he spent to get her out of Dachau. Then the manager will give her a job in his armament factory.

When Doctor Josef explains the plan to Helena, she breaks down, again, and bawls that she does not want to leave me. Then she begins whimpering for her mother. I understand her pain and longing for her mother, but truthfully, I never had the chance to experience closeness with my own mother or my stepmother. As a result, I cannot share her deep feelings. This makes me sad.

I can understand Helena being afraid of change, and I try comforting her by saying that everything will turn out just fine. I also make it clear that she can always visit me on weekends. I also remind her that the doctor's decisions are based on what he believes is in our best interests, so she must thank him and do well at her factory job.

Lou Ellen

In less than a week, Helena left the hospital and began work at one of the many outlying factories whose work supported the war effort. Moreover, Katerina moved from her temporary hospital room into the home of Dr. Josef and his wife Gerta, who prepared a living space for Katerina upstairs. Furnishings included a single bed, small desk, a bedside table, two lamps for reading, and a water closet. She will join the couple for meals downstairs.

In due time, Gerta explained that she and her husband had a grown daughter who was serving with the regular German forces. They have received no word from their only child in months, and they were very concerned for her safety.

Katerina

Right away, I like the doctor's wife very much. She is slim, beautiful, and has the look of a typical German woman with her blonde hair and blue eyes. When she walks nearby, I love the flower garden fragrance that surrounds her. She is also friendly, warm, and understanding. She keeps insisting I call her Gerta, which I must remind myself to do, while Dr. Josef wants me to call him Poppa. The truth is I am very happy here. I dream at night that Gerta is my dear mother, Poppa is my kind father, and I am living a wonderful life.

In my closet upstairs, I have nothing but Dachau's hand-me-down clothes, so immediately, Gerta says when she has some spare time, she will go up in the attic and bring down a load of her daughter's outfits. No more than two or three days pass when she brings down an armload full and says, "Katerina. Be sure you pick out whatever you like. Wash them, wear them, and say nothing else." Next, she opens a drawer and hands me a pair of fancy—no, gorgeous—handmade gloves with decorative stitching around the edges and tiny white buttons sewn on top. They are the color of sand and are soft as baby skin. Oh my. These gloves are too beautiful to give away, but Gerta insists I have them. This touches me beyond any words I can say, except a poor thank you. I also thank God for connecting me with her and Poppa. Because of this wonderful German couple, I am alive and well.

In no time, Gerta decides to fatten me up by cooking a special breakfast.

Lou Ellen

She encouraged Katerina to eat generous portions of toast, butter, jam, and hot cereal. Gerta also recommended that Katerina wash down the hearty meal with a locally produced beer. "This is what we call *Schwartz bier* or black beer," Gerta explained, as she placed a stein in front of her filled with heady brew. "With your first swallow, you will notice it has a coffee or chocolate flavor I know you will like. Both Josef and I enjoy a glass with every meal, but for you, my dear, Schwartz bier will help you plump up and fill out."

Accordingly, on most weekends, when Katerina was free from work, Gerta prepared her a meal at 10:00 a.m. known as *fristook*. It consisted of a fried egg placed on top of a butter-slathered slice of bread. As usual, Gerta served Katerina generous amounts of black beer with the meal.

Katerina

At suppertime, Gerta gives me extra portions of meat, which never seems enough. In the beginning, both Poppa and Gerta warn me against eating too much too soon. Several times, though, I overeat and wind up with a bellyache and throwing up. Sometimes I keep eating even when I feel full, and I know this must stop. Poppa calls this the "starvation ailment."

Lou Ellen

Consequently, within six months, Katerina looked and felt like a new person. Her former dull blonde hair turned sleek and gorgeous. Her chalk-like blotchy complexion became clear and baby-skin smooth. Her cheeks even sported a rosy tinge, she recalled. In addition, she gained weight and grew taller. The former was significant but not excessive. Gerta characterized Katerina's appearance as "just right" and told her it was time to cut back on the beer and extra food.

In addition to her new healthy appearance was Katerina's sense of security and contentment. She delighted in the weekend visits of her friend, Helena, who usually had time off from her work at the armament factory. She arrived by train, and the two spent Saturdays and Sundays together upstairs, chatting about the past, ambling along the paths of a nearby forest, or strolling around the hospital grounds.

Toward year's end, just as Katerina was settling down comfortably with her hospital work and living arrangements, Dr. Josef informed Kate, as he then affectionately called her, that he had something important to tell her. Similarly, Kate renamed her benefactor, Poppa Jo, because she declared, he was "the best poppa in the whole wide world."

The doctor went on informing her that his assignment at the hospital was nearly finished, and his new orders required moving to Stuttgart.

Katerina

When Poppa Jo, first gives me the news, tears come to my eyes, and my stomach tightens in a hard knot. Then my hands shake so much, I hold them behind my back. What will happen to me now? Where will I go? Suddenly, it dawns on me that I am having the same fear as Helena about leaving. I am speechless, but before I can collect my thoughts, Poppa Jo gives me a big hug. "Don't worry, Kate," he says as he tries reassuring me. "You are going with us. Do not forget that I pay good money for you, and you will continue working with me at the medical facility in Stuttgart. Again, Gerta and I will provide your room and board, so you see, nothing will change except our surroundings." All the time Poppa is explaining everything, I am thinking, *Oh my gosh, what will happen to Helena?*

Lou Ellen

Prior to the move to Stuttgart, Helena spent another weekend with Katerina in Poppa and Gerta's home. The entire time, Katerina fretted over how and when she would break the news to her Czech friend. She knew the task would be difficult for them both.

Katerina

Helena and I always have a good time when she visits. I often wonder where she finds the money for train tickets, but I don't ask.

This is a lesson I learn well at Dachau—eyes to the ground and mouth closed. See nothing, hear nothing, and say nothing. Besides, where she comes up with train money is not my business, so we look back at our time in Dachau, and chat about our jobs here. Helena says her position, sorting parts for small arms and machine guns, is so dull and boring she has to pinch herself to keep from daydreaming. "The floor boss is always yelling at me to work faster," she adds. "At least, it is much better than hospital work." We have a long discussion about Hitler, the Third Reich, the end of the war, and our plans for the future. Helena then asks, "What makes Hitler so vicious? Why do you think his SS men follow his every word?"

"I'm not positive, Helena," I tell her. "But I am wondering if Hitler did not have nasty parents who whipped his butt whenever he did something wrong, and he listened to their insults and put-downs all his young life. Then as an adult, the people listen to his ideas about a pure German race, and he makes all kinds of promises that his compatriots believe he can keep. His power builds, and eventually it goes to his head. By now, he sees himself as some sort of savior. He gets away with ruthless and spiteful acts, and in time, he forgets the difference between right and wrong—or else he just doesn't give a rip."

Then I ask for Helena's thoughts on the reason Hitler's SS men follow his orders without question. "Well," she says, "the easy answer is that they think they will be shot. Otherwise, it seems most of these people are cowards, afraid to say boo to a bug. Where are the brave ones who will stand up and be counted?"

Lou Ellen

Eventually, the two friends discussed their plans once the war ended. Helena questioned Katerina regarding her hospital work and asked whether she would return to Poland and seek some sort of medical related position. Katerina told her she would like to become a nurse or midwife, but she would need additional training. Above all, she stressed that she doubted she would ever return to Poland.

Helena admitted she was so homesick for her family and every-day life in Czechoslovakia that she could hardly wait until the time came when she finally returned home. In addition, she revealed to Katerina that she frequently woke up crying in the middle of the night from a recurring dream. In her nightmare, she was in her own country naked, screaming in terror, and running from a man dressed in a black uniform. He bolted after her with a dagger in his hand and chased her to the edge of a cliff. There she had to select from two choices: stop and die from stab wounds on homeland soil, or take a chance and jump over the ledge to a foreign country, where she hoped, miraculously, that she would land safely and begin a new life. Before she decided which route to take, she suddenly woke up sweating and sobbing.

Katerina

I explain to Helena what I think is the meaning of her dream. Without question, she will return to Czechoslovakia, provided she can hang on until the war is over. Her nightmare is telling her that choices are not always easy or safe, and sometimes, you have no choice except taking a risk.

Helena then asks me what kind of risk I am willing to take. "That is, if you do not go back to Poland. Where will you go, huh?" She keeps pushing for an answer, driving me nuts. At this point, I do not have the slightest idea and tell her it is too early for making a decision. When I know the answer, she will be the first person to know.

By now, I figure it is high time to get down to business with Helena and break the news that I am leaving Berlin. First, I must lighten the mood, so I grab her hands, and we prance around in circles and sing silly little songs. When we are laughing like fools and I can hardly catch my breath, my prediction is that she will meet a rich, dark and handsome Czech man. When the war ends, the two will fall passionately in love. Within a year, they will have a huge wedding, and in nine months, she will give birth to their first child, a boy. Thereafter, she and her man will produce a cart full of beautiful children. She breaks out in a smile. I know she loves a picture I have created. I hope it comes true.

Finally, I inform her that Poppa, Gerta, and I are leaving Berlin and relocating to Stuttgart. We hug, kiss, shed tears, and repeat good wishes and good-byes. Helena surprises me. She does not break out crying and carrying on. How come? I ask her. She grins and says proudly, "I don't cry that much anymore, Katerina. I handle things much better than I used to." Suddenly, it crosses my mind that I see her in a new light: mature and strong. I am proud of her.

At the door, we give each other our word—no matter what happens, we promise to keep in touch. Once Helena goes out the door, though, I cannot help wondering if we will.

Lou Ellen

Katerina realized that day in and day out living often buried promises and good intentions. However, she knew as time passed by, vows and expectations frequently hid in secret places as the consequence of receding or vanished memories. Nevertheless, Katerina convinced herself it would never happen to her, and she promptly erased it from her mind.

Two days later, Katerina left Berlin with Dr. Josef and his wife. Thus began the trio's 350-mile journey to Stuttgart, a large industrial city located in southwest Germany.

Stuttgart

Lou Ellen

In the summer of 1944, the US 8th Air Force and the Royal Air Force continued bombing the city as they have done so since 1940, attempting to destroy Stuttgart's significant infrastructure. The raids obliterated automobile factories such as Daimler and Porsche, military bases, and rail transportation. However, resulting damage to Stuttgart was proving less effective as it was with other German cities. For one reason, the city spread outward in deep valleys, which made such structures difficult for bombing crews to identify. Secondly, the sides of the surrounding hills contained many deep bomb shelters.

It was in the city's deep valley that the *kriegslazarett* or general hospital was located. One of Hitler's various organizations was assisting the German Armed Forces manage the facility. It was there that Katerina and Dr. Josef would work. He explained to Katerina that at this hospital, patients with major compound fractures, brain injuries, and chest wounds would undergo surgery. He said, "In other words, Kate, the most seriously wounded soldiers are brought here. We are prepared to handle more than two hundred patients, so you'll find yourself plenty busy."

Katerina

I live upstairs in a big house that Poppa Jo and Gerta rent. It is only two blocks away from the hospital. Poppa says we are quite safe from bombing because our workplace looks like a group of apartment buildings. There is also a prisoner-of-war compound nearby,

93

and Poppa says the allies are reluctant to destroy a POW camp holding men of many nationalities. My hospital job here is much different from the one in Berlin. For one thing, the soldiers' battle wounds are more severe and traumatic. The blind men insist on washing themselves. When they hear my young-lady voice, they say, "Listen, sweetie or honey, just lead us to the showers and then leave. When we finish, we will wrap towels around us and call you for assistance. Then you can help us dress above the waist. We will take care of the bottom half." It is fine with me, I say.

It doesn't take long before I figure out that some patients appreciate me, and some do not. One guy is very nasty. He has a foul mouth and constantly complains to Poppa about me. He insists I play favorites and work more with them than I do with him, and he says, "It just isn't fair." I come right out in front of Poppa and tell him he is so full of bull crap, it is running out his ears. Poppa listens patiently as Dirty Mouth keeps up the attack. Poppa turns to me. I shake my head; it is not true. Poppa orders the soldier out of the room and advises him to stay away until he behaves and cleans up his act. I feel good. Poppa Jo has confidence I am doing a good job, and now I will have a little peace and quiet. I am happy he is gone.

Lou Ellen

Daily, Katerina looked outdoors from the second floor hospital window on her way to the dining area, sometimes stopping for a few minutes to watch prisoners working out, playing games, or just ambling around in the exercise yard below. Other employees followed suit, especially young nurses, who caught the men's attention.

Katerina

Some women smile and wave; others blow kisses. One or two nurses use hand motions and body movements, showing their friendship, sympathy, and hopefully, the beginning of some form of communication. Oftentimes, the POWs draw attention to themselves with loud whistling, singing songs, and making weird noises and sounds. Well, I watch these poor prisoners, young and middle-aged, ambling around the enclosure, looking thin and sickly, depressed and sad. I begin thinking. Finally, I come up with a plan. Later, I go to the kitchen, where I approach this nice, friendly German woman who, I believe, is the head cook. After taking her aside, we chat a bit, and then I lay it out.

"Look at the prisoners down there," I say. "They must be half starving." I ask her if we can give them the leftover food that kitchen help throws away. I make a promise that if she lets me have it, I will find a way they will receive it. "Oh, no," she whispers. "Don't cause trouble. I absolutely cannot do this. I will be beaten, stomped on, or shot. So will you."

I decide to talk the situation over with Poppa and ask his advice. I also pass on the cook's warning. Finally, I try convincing Poppa Jo that it doesn't make sense tossing good food out when hungry bony men need it, especially prisoners of war. Next, I let him know that the kitchen help tosses out leftovers in the garbage every day. I ask why we aren't giving it to the men who badly need it.

Well, the next day, Poppa gives me the okay, but I do not know exactly how to do this, I confess. "Follow me to the kitchen," he says, so I tag along behind him. First, he checks the pots and pans still setting on the stove with leftover food the cooks or cleanup workers pitch in the garbage. Then he suggests that the help scrape up and dump all the food into a bucket. While they are working at that, he rounds up bunches of old electrical cords, straps, and pieces of rope. Once he ties them together, he attaches one end to the food bucket. I do not say anything else and I go back to work.

Lou Ellen

Dr. Josef led Katerina to the window and suggested she lower the pail to the ground. Further, he instructed her to pick up scraps of bread left on tables and pop them into paper bags. "Once the good scraps are gone," he suggested, "pull the pail back up and send down the bread in another container."

Katerina lowered the first bucket from the balcony window, which dropped just inside the compound fence. A wide-eyed captive, who stood nearby, quickly backed up to the pail and shielded it from view. When the immediate area was clear of guards, several men gathered around. The container was untied, hustled away, and Katerina hauled the slack rope upward. When she received the all-clear signal, Katerina lowered the bread scraps.

Katerina

While I am passing down the food, the German kitchen workers give me dirty looks, just as if I am doing something terribly wrong. At the same time, they whisper back and forth. It is clear they do not like what I am doing. Poppa asks them what they are whispering about. They pretend they do not hear. I have no doubt, I warn Poppa, that these same women will throw food in the garbage behind my back.

Lou Ellen

Dr. Josef assured her not to worry, and he immediately penned a note and attached it to the memo board, indicating that no one was to throw anything edible in the garbage. Instead, all leftovers are given to Katerina. She has his permission to pass the scraps on to the POWs. He signed the notice, Josef L. Bayer, Lieutenant Colonel and General Surgeon Corps.

Katerina

I go to the window the next day and look down at a tall prisoner with dark hair standing there like a statue. He walks back and forth one or two times, then stops and bends over, holding his both sides with his hands. It looks like he is having trouble catching his breath. Just as I am ready to lower the filled bucket, this handsome guy, straightens back up and starts speaking in Italian to me. "Hey, young lady," he says. "What is in your pail?"

"Something to eat," I answer.

He thanks me several times. "We are glad to help," I say, turning around and moving away from the window.

This same man never shows up in the exercise yard again, so I figure he is either very sick or dead. Then one day, a week or two later, as Poppa Jo and I are finishing lunch, we suddenly hear loud whistling coming from the open window. Somebody is whistling an unfamiliar tune, but it sounds so beautiful it nearly brings tears to my eyes. It touches me so, I ask Poppa if I can see who the whistler is, and he says, "Sure, Kate, go ahead."

Well, it turns out the whistler is the same prisoner who speaks Italian. I ask if everything is okay, how he is, and other small talk, when he starts asking personal questions. "Young lady," he asks, "do you have a husband?" I am thinking this man has a lot of nerve. Still, I don't mind. I break out laughing. I tell him no. "Do you have a boyfriend, then?"

"Heavens no," I answer.

"How old are you?"

"Old enough to know better and too young to care," I say.

He answers, "You are way too old for me, so good-bye. Now I am really ticked off. I end this conversation, telling him that he is crazier than a sack full of monkeys, so he can buzz off. What a surprise it is when he comes to the drop area every day now, and I learn more about him. His name is Pitor Russo, and he is from Torre del Greco in Italy. He asks how I understand a few Italian words. I pick most of them up from our Italian neighbors and their kids in Poland, I explain. "Besides," I add, "I have a good ear for learning languages."

Suddenly, he breaks into a birdcall and begins whistling a very lovely tune. Later that day, Poppa says, "Kate, I bet your new Italian friend has a wonderful voice also."

Lou Ellen

In time, Katerina asked Pitor if he was as good at singing as he was at whistling, but he answered her negatively. Nevertheless, she said she praised his talent and told him that Dr. Josef believed he was "a decent man who had strength for overcoming hardship."

Katerina

I also pass along to him Poppa's advice: "When the war is over, you should look for a job singing, whistling, or doing something else musical. He doesn't doubt that a nice handsome man like you will make very good money—and the women will love you." Pitor just laughs.

*   *   *

From time to time, after a food drop, we chat back and forth and learn more about each other. He surprises me when he first starts calling me *sweetheart* and finally gives me a reason for poo-pooing Poppa's postwar job suggestion. I remember Pitor's exact words: "Listen, sweetheart, this wound near my heart will not allow me to sing, or do much of anything else. I have trouble breathing and when I bend over, I sometimes get dizzy."

Oh my gosh. Now I am his sweetheart. Is he serious? My heart is pounding like an angry drummer. He looks up. In the sunlight, his eyes are as blue and clear as a calm sea. "I'm sorry about your wound" is all I can think to say. He begins talking again, but his words stumble. Then, "Katerina, sweetheart. I am telling you now. You are going to marry me. I mean…no. I am asking you. Will you marry me?"

"Are you crazy?" I ask him, laughing. Actually, I have mixed emotions. I am happy, scared, and have a strange warm feeling that I cannot describe. Up to this point, it seems my whole life is filled with fear and worry. Every day, I pray to God that one day my life will become much better. I often ask myself, "Will I ever know true happiness and joy? Ever be happy?" Right now, I'm fighting an attack of the blues. Even so, I haven't lost hope. Still, I am sick and tired of holding my tongue, watching my back, keeping cautious, remaining on guard, kowtowing, and kissing everybody's behind. I am leery of everyone except Poppa and Gerta. The biggest question is, do I dare trust this good-looking dark wounded Italian?

Lou Ellen

Meanwhile, weeks turned into months, and the daily food transfer plan operated without a hitch. Even the kitchen staff cooperated. Katerina and Pitor took advantage of every opportunity to contact each other and talk. During her free time, Katerina occasionally walked outdoors from the hospital and ambled along the prison camp fence. Oftentimes, Pitor would come out of his barrack, and the pair enjoyed a few minutes chatting. Pitor also made certain he stationed himself near the fence when Katerina and Dr. Josef finished their hospital shift and began their walk home. On those occasions, the doctor strolled ahead of Katerina and reminded her to "take your time and catch up when you finish."

Katerina

Before long, I am thinking Poppa has the idea that things are getting serious between Pitor and me because Poppa asks me to inform my Italian friend that he has arranged with prison officials for Pitor to come into the hospital the next day for a medical exam. I ask Poppa how he could arrange this.

"You will see, Kate," he answers in his deep voice. "I want that stocky SS officer—the one you are not fond of—to bring Pitor over here."

"No, Poppa Jo," I argue, "please."

He insists I steal syringes and makes up other lies, hoping I will quit or lose my job. Again, I plead with Poppa, asking him if he wants Pitor dead. Then I argue that if this SS grizzly shows up in a fighting mood, nothing will stop him from eliminating my friend and me. Well, Poppa tries convincing me this will never happen. Speaking softly, I guess to calm me down, he says, "My dear Kate. I repeat. Do not worry. I always carry a holstered pistol under my trouser leg. If he tries anything funny, I will shoot him first." Still, I am afraid. My hands shake. Finally, after I calm down a bit, I remember the words of a common Polish saying, reciting it to Poppa: "From a pitcher, God pours life into death, then death into life, and He does not spill a drop."

The point I am trying to make, I explain to Poppa, is that I will not interfere with God's plan for Pitor's life. Once more, I explain that this SS officer cannot stand the sight of me. I practically get down on my knees, begging Poppa to find another person to accompany Pitor to the hospital for his medical exam.

Lou Ellen

Again, Dr. Josef tried calming her fear. He told her he was pleased with her work ethic; she got along with everyone, and he knew she was honest and would not steal. He then repeated that she must trust him when he told her nothing would happen to her or her Italian friend. Katerina remained silent, but she told me she remained unconvinced.

The following morning, the SS officer directed Pitor to the treatment room and greeted Katerina with a scowling grunt. He stood close to the examining table and watched her every move as she handed Pitor a sheet. She instructed him to strip and lie on the table. She would return with Dr. Josef in a few minutes, she added. When both reentered, Dr. Josef sent the SS man into the hall. He began the examination.

Katerina

With me standing by, Poppa says to Pitor, "Kate often worries about you. She thinks the SS man is hatching a plot to harm you or Kate, and she doesn't want to carry this burden."

I do not say a word. Poppa Jo keeps checking Pitor and asking questions. He listens to Pitor's chest with his stethoscope, first in front, then around his back. He instructs Pitor to hold his breath and then let it out. When Poppa finishes checking him over, he says, "I can see by the scar that you took a nasty hit to your chest. When I listen to you heart, you have a distinct murmur. Most likely, it is the result of your heart valve not closing completely. I am not certain whether your current condition and your battle wound are related. Have you had chest pain or shortness of breath? Any dizziness? No chest pain?"

Pitor answers, "No, I don't have any of that, but I do have shortness of breath quite often, and some dizziness, especially when I stand up after bending over."

Poppa nods. "Surgery on the heart is still in its infancy," he explains. "So at this point, it is not an option. In the next decade or two, however, I believe heart valve repair and replacement will become routine procedures. Meanwhile, I will prescribe medication, which should work quite well for you."

Lou Ellen

Doctor Josef instructed the SS officer to accompany Pitor to the pharmacy before returning him to the prisoner compound. After they left, Katerina thanked the doctor for going out of his way to help her friend. Then she tidied up and prepared the examination room for another patient.

That afternoon, when the physician had seen all of his patients, Katerina tackled a variety of other duties. She sterilized instruments and checked to determine whether supplies such as gauze dressings, adhesive tape, needles, and syringes, and cotton balls needed restocking. Next, she proceeded to Dr. Josef's office where she dusted shelves, emptied the wastebasket, and straightened up paperwork on his desk. Suddenly, she jumped, startled by a throaty sound causing her to whirl around. Standing there in the open doorway, glaring at her, was the SS officer who openly disliked her. Smirking, he acknowledged Katerina's presence. He aimed an imaginary pistol at her chest, bent his index finger, and at the same time, mimicked pulling the trigger by clicking his tongue against his teeth.

Katerina

Besides this, Hitler's bogeyman hacks up mucus then clears it from his throat. He even has the nerve shouting that I am "*ein schmutziges schwein*" (a dirty pig). He is the dirty, disgusting one; not me. Anyway, if he thinks I am upset and will break out bawling from his name-calling, he has another guess coming. I will not bow down to his level, so I give him my best mile-wide smile and say, "*Vielen dank, offzier.*" (Thank you, officer.) In the end, I believe politeness always wins.

Poppa Jo charges out from nowhere. He questions the SS man. "Did I hear you say that Kate is swine?" He doesn't answer. Poppa goes on. "She is as far removed from your absurd description as a clam is to a cockroach. If anyone is swine, you are." A nasty sunburn colors the trooper's face. I do not say anything else and I go back to work.

The next morning, Poppa makes a big deal out of letting me know that the SS officer is no longer at the hospital. His new assignment is at the battlefront. I do not ask for details. I am relieved he is gone. I thank Poppa and give him a quick hug.

* * *

Lou Ellen

By 1944, the war raged throughout Europe, with setbacks and advances on both sides of the conflict. Toward the end of May, German forces retreated from Anzio, Italy. In June, a Waffen SS Panzer company surrounded a small village of 625 inhabitants in West-Central France, and approximately 400 men were forced inside several barns and garages. Soldiers then drove over 200 women and children inside the Catholic church and locked the doors. Then the order was given: "Light the fires!" Almost every person inside burned alive. One or two individuals who stumbled outdoors were mowed down by machine-gun fire. In addition, Germans launched their first V-1 rocket against Great Britain in June. In August, the Gestapo arrested Anne Frank and her family in Holland, and two months later in October, Hitler ordered Field Marshall Erwin Rommel's death. He believed Rommel was involved in the unsuccessful plot to kill him. The führer gave Rommel two choices: face a tribunal or commit suicide. The probable consequence of a tribunal was execution. Rommel agreed to take his own life by swallowing a cyanide pill. In return, he was told that his wife and son would remain safe from harm. Newspaper articles indicated that the popular Africa corps officer died from wounds he was currently recovering from when Allied aircraft strafed his command car, which occurred weeks earlier. The true story came out in the Nuremberg trials.

Early in 1945, Allied ground troops advanced toward Stuttgart. The city and its inhabitants were in constant state of confusion and upheaval. Before long, hundreds of war-weary foot soldiers and storm troopers deserted and fled the city. Katerina and the doctor remained at their hospital jobs, but the surgeon admitted to Katerina that their working days there were numbered. He also revealed that he and Gerta would soon leave Stuttgart and move to his family farm, whose location was twenty miles from the city.

Katerina

With all this craziness going on, Poppa Jo and Gerta urge me to think about my future. They suggest I marry a fine man. Gerta adds, "Pitor seem like a good choice, don't you agree, Katerina?"

For several days, I think Gerta's suggestion over. I pray often and ask God to give me some kind of answer. Pitor and I talk about marrying every time we get together. I never will forget his words. "You and me," he says, "have been through hell. We deserve all the happiness we can find right now. Don't you agree?" He goes on melting my heart when he says, "Listen, sweetie. I want you to be my wife and mother to our children. I will love you, and only you, until I draw my last breath. After the war is over, we will live anywhere you want. We made it this far, so the rest should be sheer heaven. Yes?"

I tell you the truth. I pray twice a day asking God for guidance so I will make the right decision. Until the time comes, though, I must weigh the advantages and disadvantages. Both sides need weighing. I am certain Pitor is a good, honest, and faithful man. For these reasons alone, I have no problem marrying him. On the other hand, imagining marriage scares me. What happens if I misjudge his character? Am I miserable the rest of my life? All the hunger, hurting, pain, sickness, and dying, I want to forget. On the other hand, I have a bellyful of name calling (dirty swine) and put-downs (worthless as tits on a boar, or worthless as a horse with no legs). Misery follows wherever I go, it seems, so I will make one promise I will not break. I will never set foot in Poland again. It is the place where pain and punishment leaves an ugly scar on my heart and soul.

* * *

Lou Ellen

After Katerina spent a week or two mulling over Pitor's proposal and listened to the doctor's urging, Katerina agreed to marry her sweetheart. Her future husband was beside himself with joy, my friend recalled. Gerta, who was also delighted with the decision, announced that wedding preparations would begin at once. She and her husband would take care of every detail. "Neither of you should worry about a single thing," she added. Katerina said she started protesting, but Gerta cut her short. "Listen, you two," she began lecturing. "You both have shown strength and endurance to survive pushing, kicking, pistol whipping, starvation, degradation, and heaven knows what else. Dr. Josef and I want to do all we can to make up for some of it, so let us start planning now. How would you like a nice postwedding dinner party?"

Katerina

Poppa Jo and Gerta's generosity is so overwhelming, I am silent. I have no words that describe the love and gratitude I have for them. Instead, I thank them over and over again—a poor substitute for describing my deep feelings.

Pitor makes praying hands and bows down. He begins speaking in German and then switches to his native Italian, expressing his thanks and appreciation for all they do for us. In Italian, he says he will never forget their kindness. I doubt if they understand everything he says in his native tongue, but they look and act as if they do.

In the afternoon, I go along with Gerta when she visits the local butcher. She explains that she requires good meat for the wedding dinner, but she has no ration stamps with which to give him. The butcher wipes his hands over his stained apron and smiles. *"Das macht nichts,"* (it doesn't matter) he states cheerfully. "You are my best customer, Gerta, so this is my plan. I will kill my number four pig, the one I always hide away in a safe place. If the SS come back again, and their records show I still own three pigs, I am okay. What they do not know will not hurt them. Ha ha. There is more than one way to trick these ugly SS buzzards."

*　*　*

Lou Ellen

Now that the Third Reich began crumbling, prison guards abandoned their posts at the POW camp adjacent to the hospital and many captives scattered. Immediately, Dr. Josef arranged for Pitor to move into a vacant hospital room. He also found him a job transporting patients on gurneys and performing light tasks such as sweeping, dusting, and scrubbing sinks.

In the interim, Greta enlisted the aid of friends and her husband's trustworthy colleagues for rounding up additional items for the wedding dinner: potatoes, fresh bread, root vegetables, and beer. In addition, Gerta intended to bake a fancy cake for the affair.

Many nights prior to the ceremony, Gerta stayed up past midnight, cutting material, making alterations, and stitching some of her daughter's skirts, dresses, and underwear for the future bride.

Katerina

All this sewing takes a lot of Gerta's time. Her daughter's clothes are a much larger size than I wear, so there is more work for her to make everything fit correctly. I feel guilty when I see her staying up late at night sewing, but at the same time, I am very happy. She is such a sweetheart.

Finally, the big day arrives. Poppa's boyhood friend, Franz Bernard, now a priest, will marry us at home with Poppa and Gerta acting as our witnesses. All morning, Pitor and I get ready for the afternoon ceremony. My soon-to-be husband looks very handsome with his shiny black hair slicked back from his forehead, instead of his usual stringy, scruffy look. Also, his face looks different—younger, maybe—with his floppy mustache shaved off.

Pitor's wedding outfit is on loan from Poppa: gray trousers, white shirt, bright-red tie, and a dark blue suit jacket, all very rich-looking.

As for myself, well, I feel beautiful inside and out. My wedding gown is pure white with long sleeves, and it has a nice bow in the back. Gerta says she wore the dress one time at a fancy ball, and she has not put it on since. After she added a little lace and made other additions, Gerta presents me with a beautiful wedding dress. It fits perfectly.

As if this kind and extremely generous couple haven't done enough, they give us family treasures as wedding gifts. Gerta hopes that Pitor will accept her late mother's gold band for slipping it on my finger during the ring exchange part of the ceremony. "This ring," she adds, "looks rather plain, but it is an yellow-gold 18-carat beauty celebrating your new wife and a new life to come." Pitor thanks her in German and accepts her gift with a huge hug and a noisy kiss.

In the meantime, Poppa has trouble untying the strings on a small red velvet pouch. When it finally comes open, he reaches in and pulls out bold-looking man's ring. "For years, I wore this old gem every day without taking it off," he says. "But for the past few years, I cannot make it fit over the middle knuckle on my ring finger. Therefore, it is now yours to present to your groom with the hope that you two will have a happy and lifelong union." He points out the details: an18-carat white gold band mounted with black onyx gemstone. Atop the stone is a flying eagle, also made of white gold. Why, it is loveliest piece of jewelry I have ever seen, and while I am thanking both Poppa and Gerta for their presents, I cannot believe this sudden turnabout will last.

Lou Ellen

In due time, Father Bernard arrived at Dr. Josef's place, and the wedding ceremony began shortly afterward. First, he gave a short homily on the sanctity of marriage, emphasizing that it is a lifelong commitment interrupted only by death. Subsequently, when the couple affirmed their vows and exchanged rings, the holy father offered his blessing and pronounced them husband and wife.

"You may now kiss your bride, Pitor," Father Bernard coached. The groom's face flushed. He hesitated. Katerina said she held her breath. He did not disappoint her. He planted a long passionate kiss. The priest smiled. Once the couple and their witnesses signed the required legal papers, the wedding party and invited guests ambled toward the spacious dining room where a celebration dinner was planned.

Katerina

After Poppa and Gerta introduce to us their friends and associates, we head inside the dining room. Watching friendly people milling around in high spirits and listening to loud laughter indicates everyone is ready for a bang-up celebration; so are my husband and me. At this instant, I am on top of the world, and Pitor, who cannot keep his eyes off me, is constantly beaming like a sun dog.

Lou Ellen

After having chatted with the newlyweds, Father Bernard expressed regret that he was unable to stay for the reception dinner because of a prior commitment: visiting battle-weary and severely wounded warriors in the medical wards. The newlyweds thanked him for his service and said they were sorry he could not stay but understood.

Subsequently, as Pitor and Katerina entered the room, their eyes fixed on a decorated oblong table on the left side. Two crystal vases that held trumpet-shaped white flowers were placed at each end. The centerpiece consisted of a large bouquet containing ferns and a variety of pink and white flowers. Flickering on each side were lighted white tapers placed in silver candlesticks. A smaller circular table, placed on the opposite right side, held a three-layer wedding cake that Gerta baked earlier. Swirled white frosting covered the creation, and handpicked blue flowers adorned the tiers.

Additionally, the main dining table featured eighteen-place settings, consisting of Gerta's fine Dresden china while guests continued mingling around the room admiring the decorations. All the while, Gerta and her helpers scurried from kitchen to table with hot food. At once, luscious aromas permeated the room: roast pork, root vegetables, thyme, sage, and other spices. Steam rose from two bowls filled with mashed potatoes and topped with melted butter. Hot dark-brown sauce filled a pair of gravy boats, and heated platters were piled with generous slices of roasted pork.

Once the guests found their assigned seats, someone suggested that everyone toast the newlyweds first, then their hosts. That said, he rose, flipped the hinged thick metal wire up and over the white ceramic top on the beer bottle, paused, and poured the brew into his stein. Other celebrants followed suit.

Katerina

What a sight! All guests lifting brightly colored ceramic steins, then reaching across the table, tapping other containers, and shouting *"proist"* in unison. Pitor and I toast each other too in celebration of our new life together and the promise of a happy future. I am overwhelmed with joy. We are now one. From this day on, we are Katerina and Pitor Russo.

Honestly, though, I am very sad and disappointed that my friend, Helena, from our Dachau days, is not here to share my joy and meet my new husband. Poppa Jo says he will explain her absence later. He says he does not want to spoil our special day.

It seems like I can never thank Poppa enough for buying my way out of Dachau, and I cannot even begin to describe how kind, loving, and accepting Gerta is to an outsider like me, a once petrified Polish girl. From the beginning, she opens her home and heart to me without stalling or dragging her feet. My husband and I will always love and remember Poppa and Gerta the rest of our lives. I am as certain of this as I am of sundown.

Lou Ellen

Meanwhile, Allied ground troops continued their advance and reached Stuttgart in April 1945. French forces joined the US Seventh Army, and the two armies attacked the city with heavy artillery and bombing. Mass confusion and panic reigned. Hordes of natives wandered aimlessly among streets choked with debris. They appeared lost. Families with children picked through rubble looking for water and something to eat. Other people dug and poked through building ruins, searching for lumber, bricks, or other materials suitable for rudimentary shelter. Then, with a sense of urgency, Dr. Josef outlined his plan to the newlyweds. Until he and his wife left Stuttgart and returned to the family farm, he suggested that Katerina and her husband remain living in the apartment upstairs so long as they continued to assist him at the hospital. Both Katerina and Pitor agreed and expressed their deep-felt gratitude.

On April 21, a French armored division captured Stuttgart. They encountered little resistance. Rumors flew like a flock of noisy crows: soldiers were starving for women and sex. The word was "Keep your guard up at all times. Be careful."

Katerina

Everybody here at the hospital is afraid. Poppa does not want Pitor or me to go anywhere by ourselves. We work with Poppa and go home with him. No place else. He tells incoming soldiers that I am his daughter who has a new husband, so I am hands-off. I also hear him lose his temper at another young trooper who has no respect, but he has a big mouth. Poppa yells, "If you even touch my daughter or anyone else who works here, I will inject you with a special drug. Then you will never sleep with a woman again. Do I make myself absolutely clear?"

Toward the end of the month, the exciting news is that Hitler commits suicide in Berlin. A few days later, German forces surrender in Italy. Then on May 7 comes the news that all of us, and probably the whole world, holds its breath for: all the German troops surrender to the Allies, and the war is finally over. We whoop, holler, and dance around the dining room table. Poppa goes and brings back a bottle of his finest wine, and we celebrate way past our bedtimes. Straightaway, we finish off two more bottles of Riesling. Between sips, Pitor puckers up his lips and whistles a merry tune. By now, I think all of us are getting a little tipsy, so we wish each other a happy and restful good night.

*   *   *

Lou Ellen

At the hospital, confusion and uncertainty was widespread. The doctor explained that restrictions were placed upon soldiers and officers because of the German high command's unconditional surrender to Allied and Red Army forces. General Eisenhower, the supreme commander of the Allied Expeditionary Forces, directed that all enemy weapons must be handed over to certain officers designated by Allied representatives. In addition, German military personnel would remain in their present positions pending further instructions.

Katerina

These new rules and checks put on the Germans by the Allies are causing Poppa to change his plans. I never see him so upset. He learns he cannot receive his military discharge until the Allied higher-ups give the okay. At first, Poppa thinks once the war ends, he will receive his military discharge. Then he and Gerta will leave Stuttgart and go live on the family farm. Many times, I hear him share with Gerta the types of work he might do once he becomes a plain citizen again. One plan is for him to open up his own medical practice in the agricultural district of his homeland. His other idea is accepting his doctor friend's offer to join his practice in a large town nearby and possibly become a partner. "As it looks now," Poppa explains, "I will have to drive my car to work at the hospital every day instead of becoming my own boss and making my own decisions. Now I am at the mercy of the occupation forces for who knows how long."

Poppa brings up another problem. He informs my husband and me that we have to move out of the apartment upstairs and find another place to live. He also says we no can work at the hospital anymore. There is more bad news. Poppa finally explains why my friend Helena didn't show up at our wedding celebration. "I try telephoning the armament factory in Berlin where your friend began working," he explains. "And the operator comes on the line and says the phone is either out of order or is disconnected. Next, I get in touch with one of my former colleagues at the hospital who advises me that the plant closed its doors several months ago. This is all I know, Kate. I am very sorry."

Goodness. I just hope and pray she is still alive and safe. I am almost afraid to ask this next question, but I go ahead anyway. "Well," I say, "what about your own daughter, Poppa? Have you heard anything new?" He tells us he is constantly checking on her whereabouts, but he cannot receive a straight answer from anyone. It is painful hearing him say, "Gerta and I are beginning to lose hope for her safe return. All we can do now is pray."

There is no doubt that Poppa and Gerta are convinced their daughter is dead—probably during combat. I know she was sent to the Western front fighting the Red Army. Not knowing what happened to your only daughter must be horrifying for them. Honestly,

I cannot even imagine losing your own child. After all, parents are supposed to pass away first, not before their children. This is so upside down and backward.

Now as I sense their feelings of heartbreak and, probably, loss, their faces take on most depressing looks: droopy sad eyes and scowl lines between their brows. When the sunlight hits Gerta's face, I can even spot tiny map-like wrinkles lining her cheeks. In a flash, memories of convent life come flooding back. Even after all these years, I recall eating meals on those dull china plates, scarred with nicks and cracks.

*   *   *

Lou Ellen

In the days ahead, when all the kisses, hugs, and good-byes were said and done, Dr. Josef took the newlyweds aside, handed them four hundred German marks (equivalent to four hundred dollars) and offered his advice. "Food is scarce, and it will probably become worse," he said. "But if you have money, you will manage. Buy just enough food to keep yourselves alive—and watch your spending. Determine the number of marks you need just to get by and stick with it. Be resourceful. It will save your lives. I have done my upmost to keep Pitor healthy, yet I have no idea what the future will bring—his, yours, or ours. Nevertheless, here is our farm address. Keep in touch and remain safe."

Following the couple's departure to the farm, Katerina and Pitor contacted Dr. Josef's former landlady and asked if they could rent her upstairs apartment. She shook her head, saying, *"Nein, nein."* Then she wagged her finger at the pair. "I want no foreigners living here. I rent the apartment only as a favor to the doctor and his wife. Now they are gone."

Katerina

My husband does not give up. "But we have the money right here," he argues, pulling the marks out of his trouser pocket.

"Nein," she replies. *"Auf, wiedersehen!"* (Good-bye!)

"Okay," Pitor says, grabbing me by the hand. "Forget her. We will find a place ourselves. Let's go."

Lou Ellen

Katerina and her husband heard there was a temporary camp where uprooted people like themselves were finding temporary shelter. They learned that the facility once functioned as a German military training camp. Its location was partially hidden in a remote wooded area outside of Stuttgart.

Katerina

When Germany surrenders, all the soldiers here flee, but before they do, the men smash everything usable to pieces. Four married couples, including my husband and me, wind up sharing living quarters in a vacant beat-up barrack. Immediately, the men scrounge around the area looking for boards, pieces of tin, and other materials to patch up doors, windows, and anything else that needs fixing. While they are busy working at these jobs, four of us women roam all over the place, first, in the woods, hunting for food. In the beginning, we find nothing, which is depressing. Then we wander out from the woods into what looks like a pasture. Someone whispers, "Look. Is that a cow?" Yes, it is a cow, but she is behind a fence. Now what? "Well," one woman asks, "who among us knows how to milk a cow quickly?" Nobody answers. Finally, I admit that I have milked plenty of cows as a kid. Naturally, they choose me to crawl under bossy and milk her, but I ask who else besides me will shimmy under the fence and milk the cow on the other side. No one answers. I ask who else has ever milked a cow. I do not hear a peep out of anyone. Finally, Granny Sippi, as we call her, says, "Me. Years ago, as a kid, and I haven't had that chore since."

"Thank goodness. This is good news." But Granny insists she doesn't remember how. I explain: "At the top of the udder, take hold of one teat. Squeeze and pull all the way down to the end at the same time. Go slow and easy, and the milk comes squirting out. If we use pails, we will work two teats at a time and finish faster." Next, I ask

Sippi if she can shimmy under the fence with me. "Don't be silly," she snaps. "Just watch me."

Lou Ellen

One woman from the group said, "Hold on a minute. For one thing, we have nothing to hold milk. Second, what happens if the farmer or one of his hands spots us out here trying to steal his milk? You know the farmhouse is not that far away from here. We should think this over. I do not want to be caught and then shot." The others agreed with her and concluded that each woman would express their concerns and hone in on possible solutions.

Still within the tree line, the group moved farther back from the pasture and hunkered down in the brush and weeds for their discussions. Eventually, everyone agreed on a plan. The strategy called for Katerina and her friend, Sippi, to remain hidden in place while the remaining women ran back toward the barrack and scoured the area for any trash piles or old dumps. They hunted for tin pails, wooden buckets, or half-gallon size or larger glass jars. Once suitable containers were found, the consensus was that the hunters return to the forest with at least two of them in hand.

Katerina

Sippi and I find what we think is a perfect hiding place, so we crouch down near an very tall old oak tree near the forest edge and take cover. All around us are small dead trees, saplings, brush, and brambles. Next, we cover ourselves with dry leaves and twigs. We wait and watch for the others to return. Sippi and I pass the time doing nothing for what seems like hours. They take forever, and we are more nervous and anxious as ever. We wonder if something is wrong. Ah, finally, Granny first catches sight of them in the dim distance. We keep hiding until they arrive close to the oak tree, then we uncover. I ask them why they took so darn long. "We scouted around every trash heap and dump until we find decent containers with lids," they explain. "It takes longer than you think. Eventually, we discover a trash pile where we poke around and dig out two large glass jars with their tops still screwed on. Lucky for us, we spot a stream nearby, so we stop and spend time cleaning the dirt and grime off inside and out. All this takes time and lots of hard work." I thank them for their success and then ask Sippi if she is ready. She nods. "All right! Let's go."

Lou Ellen

Meanwhile, the successful trash-pile searchers remained under-cover in the forest and acted as lookouts. They would warn Katerina and Sippi if anyone approached from the field, forest, farmhouse, or barn.

*   *   *

Katerina

Sippi is much older than us but not ready for the boneyard. I'm guessing from the gray streaks in her hair and the worry lines on her face that she is close to forty to forty-five years old. Even so, she is in good shape because during this raid on Bossy, she wiggles under the fence with me like a worm. Anyway, after we duckwalk while carrying our empty jars and switching arms, we must stop. It is hard on our legs. Next, we push backward on our butts. When we finally get to Bossy, and she gives us a curious cow-eye stare, we take oppo-site sides. Her udder is hard and heavy with milk. "She will be easy to milk," I whisper to Granny. Within a few minutes, two or three black and white cows are curious. They wander over and stop several paces away, which places us in a safer situation. Now if the farmer or anyone else looks in our distant direction, I do not think he will see us messing with his animals and stealing his milk. At this point, we feel quite safe.

Quickly, we crouch to opposite sides of the cow, grabbing a teat and setting the glass jar underneath her. At first, Sippi struggles a bit and goes full blast. Great. She remembers. The jars fill fast. So far, everything works out perfectly. Oh no. Straightaway, we receive our punishment—a nose full of fresh, steaming cow poop that plops to the ground close by.

When the full containers have all the tops screwed on tight, Sippi and I hear a pleasant sound. Our ears perk up. We wait and listen. It is a whistle ending with a chirp. Is it a bird? Probably. Sippi swears the sound comes from the tree line where our women lookouts wait. Suddenly, it dawns on us. What is the warning signal? In our distraction, we did not decide. Our eyes focus on the farmhouse. A man in overalls and straw hat carrying something long over his shoulder slams the outside door and takes off toward us. Immediately, we screw the lids on tight, grab the heavy jars, slide them under the fence, and finally run as fast as our skinny legs will take us. Charging full speed ahead are our two panicky lookouts. Now it's everyone for himself.

*   *   *

Katerina

During supper that day, each one of us gulps down our portion of milk. When eight people share, there is hardly enough to whet your appetite. Even so, it tastes delicious. Pitor draws laughter when he jokes that if he swallows another drop, "This milk will leak out of my ears." All told, I can't remember a better meal than this one because we also have meat on the table. Several men fashion a snare for trapping animals, which they later skin and cook, but they refuse to tell us what we are eating. One man says, "Chirp, chirp." Someone guesses a bird. "Wrong," the men shout in unison. The next noise is "Quack, quack." Another person asks if we are eating duck meat. No. My milking partner, Sippi, begs for one last hint. Silence. Another fellow who imitates a woman's high-pitch voice pipes up with "Squeak, squeak, squeak."

"Are we eating wild rats?" a woman asks. "I hate those skittish brown buggers! I will starve first before I eat rat."

Yuk, this is disgusting. Just the thought of eating rats or mice is scrambling my stomach. In spite of our pressing the men for an answer, they will not identify the animals whose flesh we are eagerly chewing on and swallowing.

*   *   *

Since food is always in short supply, most nights when there is bright moonlight, our group goes outdoors in different directions and scouts for farmer's fields so we can nab a few potatoes, cabbage, turnips, carrots, or anything else we can find to eat. In our hearts, we know stealing is wrong, but no one brings the subject up. Personally, in the long run, I believe God and any decent German will forgive us. We steal to eat, and we eat to live.

Lou Ellen

Thus far, Katerina and her husband, along with the three couples who shared the same barrack, cared for themselves with no rules or supervision from anyone. Each woman selected a job in the kitchen such as preparing food, cooking, serving, washing dishes, and general clean-up. Men were responsible for building repair, maintenance, and supplying meat. The sharing of duties worked well for several months, but suddenly there was a drastic change.

The French army, which captured and occupied Stuttgart in 1945, transferred the city to the American military occupation zone a year later. At that time (1946), the American forces took charge of the abandoned German military training complex and quickly converted it into one of many transit camps sprouting up all over Europe to aid many thousands of displaced persons. The Americans faced many challenges. First was the influx of refugees numbering several hundreds who streamed into the Stuttgart camp. Many were half-starved, while others suffered illness and disease. The initial plan devised by the Allied Forces was to repatriate the refugees to their home countries as quickly as possible. Nevertheless, their primary concern was the ability to provide shelter, food, and basic health care.

Katerina

I will never forget the American officer who shows up. We are all scared. I do not trust any soldier. I feel better when he speaks Polish and asks how we live here by ourselves. We just shrug our shoulders. How do you explain? You do what you must.

Before the American takeover, all of us could leave the compound whenever we wanted. Now all people who go outdoors are required to wear badges on their clothing, which identifies a person's home country. For example, the letter *I* on Pitor's badge stands for Italy while mine is marked *P* for Poland. Even worse, all persons who leave the compound must sign out at the guard shack, list a destination, and a return time. It looks to me like the days of coming and going whenever you please are long gone.

* * *

Lou Ellen

One day, when Katerina sat in the office filling out her registration papers among a group of others, an administrator asked if anyone present could translate from one language to another, and, if so, in which language was he or she most proficient.

Katerina

I raise my hand. I can speak the Ukrainian language plus Polish, Russian, German, and Czech. I only know a little Italian, I tell her. For one thing, all these languages are similar. Then, too, I pick up different languages easier than most people. After I am the only one raising my hand, the office lady asks me to come over to her. "I have just the job for you," she says.

"But I do not want a job," I argue.

"We will pay you one mark for every hour you work translating. How does that sound?" I think about it and decide the pay is better than nothing, so I agree.

Lou Ellen

Katerina's first assignment was translating for a Ukrainian woman. It goes so smoothly the woman in charge suggested that Katerina think about working every day. "This will mean more income for you," she said, "and perhaps even a pay raise." Katerina decided she would try.

Katerina

During the day, I translate for another Ukrainian, a Pole, and a couple of Czechs, helping them with their registration forms until I am worn-out. I tell the office worker I am so tired I need to stop working. I am going to lie down and get some sleep. Besides, I explain, I have a splitting headache. "Yes," the supervisor says. "You are turning pale. I can see you are sick. Come, I will take you to the infirmary."

Just when I am about to see the doctor, I feel my period starting. I have terrible cramps, and my back hurts so bad, I can hardly sit still. Now I feel like I am burning up. Then I am freezing to death. I describe all this to the doctor when he comes into the room. "How long ago did you have your previous menstrual cycle?" he asks.

"Three or four years," I figure.

Before he leaves, the doctor gives me medicine to take and tells me to stay in bed and rest. "If your flow becomes heavier, or your cramps worsen, be sure you let me know, all right?"

Later, my head stops aching, but I keep feeling hot, then cold. This makes me nervous because in Dachau, at different times, I watch girls during their cycle who have terrible hot and cold flashes. The next thing you know, their bodies begin shaking all over, and they wind up dying. I do not want this to happen to me, and I am worried it is possible.

The rest of the day is bad. The blood keeps coming, and no wants to stop. The next day is better, and on the third day, I have just a little flow, so I go back to my job. Well, before long, my back starts killing me just below the ribs. I have no choice but to quit work and rest. The office supervisor is not happy with me. "If you start this 'off again, on again sickness' business," she warns, "I will fire your fanny."

I think, *Why, you old biddy. I'm not going to take your bull.* So I quit on the spot, walk out, go back to the barrack, and lie down for a nap.

Lou Ellen

That afternoon, Pitor and several of Katerina's bunkmates urge her to return to work. At first, she refused. Her husband pointed out to her, "People are depending on you to help them, and the ones who try taking your place have an awful time translating correctly." Feeling guilty, Katerina relented and returned to the office. The first word the supervisor greeted her with was, "Oh…Katerina. Thank God, you came back ready to translate. No one can interpret different languages like you. I apologize for getting upset and angry."

*　　*　　*

Months later, Katerina discovered she was pregnant with their first child. She no longer had periods, and lately, she felt a faint flutter sensation deep inside her belly. Her husband was ecstatic after hearing the news. Joyous, Pitor yelled, "See! I say this to you many times. Life will be good. Remember? Well, Momma, what do you think we make? A boy? Or a girl?"

Katerina

All the time, after I tell Pitor I am with baby, Pitor worries about me. He is scared I will lose our child. Almost every night after I go to sleep, I have horrible nightmares. I relive the terrible times and horrible situations at Dachau, begin screaming, and wake up, still half-asleep. Then, like a crazy person, I try climbing out of bed, as if I'm trying to run away and escape until Pitor holds me back. He keeps his arms around me, holds my hands, and strokes my face until I calm down. After I am completely awake, I no can get back to sleep. All I can do is cry. It is hard imagining what life will be like away from Germany because my life is one misery after another. Will it ever change for the better? Maybe, someday, I will know the answer.

Meanwhile, I work hard at keeping busy with the translating job and making plans for the baby. By now, I only wake up with nightmares one or two times a week; most of the morning sickness is gone, and I feel much better. I begin buying little things like booties, shirts, and baby blankets. Pitor picks up a few things himself, like rattles and other little toys, but one time, he comes and says he has a present for me. I can't image what it is. "Close your eyes first and don't open them until I say it is okay," he says. "Then you can look. I hope you like it, sweetie."

Well, I open my eyes, and I cannot believe what I see. Pitor buys me a cute little rag doll with shiny black button eyes, a bright-red smiley mouth, and yellow yarn hair. "This is what you never had as a kid," he says, proud as a rooster. "So I want you to have it now." My wonderful husband and soon-to-be father plants a big kiss on my cheek. I am over the moon.

*   *   *

Lou Ellen

During this period, American military forces at Stuttgart were anxious to begin returning their charges to their home countries. However, accomplishing this was no easy task. Many refugees, including Czechs, Poles, Ukrainians, and religious groups such as undercover Jews, refused repatriation. They feared reprisals or persecution by the Soviet Union's communist government, now entrenched in their homelands.

Katerina

The US military people tell my husband he must go back to Italy and return to his navy unit. He argues that he is now married and that I am with baby. The military insists that I cannot go with him. Pitor asks if he can stay in camp until our little one is born. Then we will go back to Italy. After my husband talks with different officials, he comes to the barrack and says we have twenty-four hours to get ready, and then we must leave. He gives me the news as I am outdoors hanging laundry on the clothesline. A woman who lives in our barrack is the same size as me, so I end up leaving everything I do not possibly need for her. She gives me some of her underwear and a few nice dresses.

The next day, American soldiers take us by truck and drop us off at the *bahnhof* (train station), and soon we are on our way to Torre del Greco.

Torre Del Greco

Lou Ellen

Following a long and exhausting six-hundred-mile train ride, the couple arrived at Torre del Greco, a rural seaside resort city. It was located at the foot of Mt. Vesuvius and overlooked the Bay of Naples.

Prior to the war, the area was a popular haven for tourists who took advantage of the warm climate, fine beaches, excellent cafes, eateries, and acres of farmland and vineyards. Many of its habitants found employment in occupations connected to fishing and shipping.

Since the seventeenth century, Torre del Greco was famous for producing coral jewelry and cameo brooches. Those items bolstered the economy for many years. However, by the time Katerina and her husband arrived there at war's end, tourism declined sharply, population rapidly increased, and farmland began disappearing. Not only was the city losing its rural character, sun worshipers were discovering new playgrounds at Sorrento and other cities located along the Amalfi coast.

Katerina

Pitor can hardly believe the changes he sees after being away from home for six long years. He says, "The Krauts used Torre del Greco as an ammo dump during the war, so the Allies never let up on their heavy bombing. Look, you still can see some of the rubble and bullet holes, but I will tell you my war stories later. First, we must find a place to live."

Let me back up. On our train ride here, Pitor talks to other navy men and locals, asking if they know about any good houses or apartments in Torre del Greco for rent. One man, who says he is a retired railroad worker, suggests that Pitor should investigate a place where returning vets and their families are most welcome.

Lou Ellen

The couple had no trouble finding the villa; it was one Pitor was familiar with prior to the war. During that period, a wealthy family owned the place, but the Italian government took possession and converted it into a series of apartments, exclusively built for returning service members and their families.

Katerina and Pitor wasted no time checking the villa out. The three-story, white stucco building had a manicured lawn, plenty of olive trees planted throughout, and a large flower bed in full bloom with ornamental grasses billowing in the background.

At that time, Katerina recalled that she couldn't help but contemplate the contrast between the beautiful villa and its surrounding landscape with the ugly, destructive war and its horrible impact on so many families and individuals.

Nevertheless, the couple contacted the landlady. She pointed out that the villa's location was ideal, with many shops, stores, and eateries, within walking distance. Best of all, she enthused, was the wonderful weather, lovely sea, and sandy beaches within walking distance.

Katerina

Pitor admits that he prefers living at the villa, as opposed to residing at navy base housing in Naples, his new duty station. "I will have no problem with transportation back and forth every day," he assures me. "The base is less than ten miles from here, and buses run on time. What do you think, sweetie?"

Oh my gosh. This place is like heaven. It is perfect for the baby. Pitor and I can no believe our eyes. We look at each other. "Yah, we will be happy to rent the apartment," he tells the landlady. We are to pay her twenty-four liras every month, which we think is a very good price since it includes furnishings. She asks if we have enough money to buy food. Before we can answer, she says, "Wait one minute." A short time later, she comes back, carrying a big basket piled full of beans, pasta, bread, jelly, flour, and other basic food. In a shaky voice, she says, "You two almost lost your lives, and believe me, I hear so many bad and ugly things that go on in camps and barracks, it is sickening. I wish you two the best of luck, and if you need anything at all, no matter how small, I am right here for you."

Oh, dear Mary, mother of Jesus. I think I will die and ride a cloud to heaven. This is what I dream about every day in Germany: nice warm weather, sandy beaches, wading in the sea, lots of green trees, and sweet-smelling flowers. Think of it. Here, nobody ever beats on your door, charges inside, and points his carbine in your face, or screams that you must obey an order. If you refuse, he will beat you to a pulp or shoot you on the spot. He leaves—but not before he steals whatever he wants.

*   *   *

Lou Ellen

It was not long before the couple settled into their new apartment and were basking in their newfound privacy, freedom, and love for each other. In addition, their excitement, nervousness, and wonder surged at the impending birth of their first child.

Meanwhile, Katerina's husband reported to the base in Naples each morning, performed his job, and returned home for supper. During the day, Katerina kept busy cleaning, cooking, washing clothes, and knitting baby booties and blankets. She had not forgotten how to knit, even though she had not picked up a needle since her convent days in Horodenka, Poland.

Subsequently, in December 1946, nine months of waiting ended, and Katerina gave birth to a seven-pound, ten-ounce baby boy. His parents named him Gregorio. Four years later, a baby girl, named Valentina, joined the family. She shared her brother's dark curly hair and olive-color skin.

Katerina

Honestly, these are the two happiest and proudest moments of my whole life. For the first time ever, I now have two beautiful children who sincerely and totally love me. In Poland, I do not have this kind of love. From my stepmother, I get nothing but hair pulling, pushing, shoving, and beating. The awful screams of "stupid," "no good," and other terrible names still ring in my ears. My husband never knows ahead of time when his ship goes out to sea, so I keep a small suitcase packed with clean socks, underwear, and a few other things. I always check to make sure I pack photographs of Gregorio, Valentina, and myself in the bag for Pitor to look at.

We have no telephone at the villa, so Pitor has a plan that will let me know when he gets his orders for sea duty. "When I receive my orders," he says, "I will send a man from the base who will come to the apartment. Give him the suitcase, and he will hand it over to me before the ship leaves the harbor."

At different times, Pitor is gone for a week or more. On these voyages, he tells me that Jewish survivors of the Holocaust secretly come aboard Italian ships at night. Then they quietly sail out of the harbor and eventually stop somewhere in the middle of the sea. It is there, Pitor explains, that the people transfer to smaller boats, then are taken illegally to Palestine—only if they manage to sneak past the British boats. Otherwise, the British navy turns them back.

* * *

Lou Ellen

The six years that Katerina and Pitor lived in Torre del Greco with their growing children were filled with love and happiness. Even though money was tight on a seaman's pay, no one complained. Katerina was content staying home with the children, and she prided herself on keeping the apartment clean and neat for her husband.

Wash days were frequent and time-consuming, but in her opinion, if you loved your man and your children, a good wife kept family members clean and dressed in spotless clothing. Doing laundry began with Katerina heating water in pails on a wood-fired stove. She then poured the hot water into two galvanized tubs, one for washing clothing by hand, and the other larger tub for rinsing. Then she wrung out the dripping articles and carried the loaded basket to the terrace where she hung them on lines to dry. She washed and rinsed diapers on separate days from the family clothing. When Katerina did not wash clothing or diapers, the large galvanized container served as the family bathtub.

*　　*　　*

It was during those years living in Torre del Greco that Katerina described as pure happiness and contentment. In addition, it was the first time that her husband first shared his wartime experiences. He described how he was wounded, captured, and taken prisoner.

Katerina

My husband was nineteen-years-old when he signed up for the Italian navy, he tells me. This was in 1937, when Italy joined Germany and got into the war against the Allies. His assignment was serving on one of the navy's auxiliary vessels that transport food, supplies, and fuel from shore and out to their carriers and battleships involved in the fighting. He talks about different invasions against France, Egypt, and Greece; I can't remember the others. He goes on describing Allied operations in southern Italy, right in this area, while at the same time, Germans were attacking in the north.

All these battles are confusing, like who is fighting who, when, where, and why. "When is this?" I ask.

"Well, sweetie," he says, "it is confusing, but I will start from the beginning. In 1940, Italy joined the war with the other two countries (Germany and Japan) forming the Axis pact. Three years later, Mussolini was arrested, later killed, and our government surrendered to the Allies and signed the armistice pact. In other words, once Mussolini was out of the picture, we joined with United States, Russia, Great Britain, and others. Not long afterward, we joined the Allied Forces against the Axis. During the fighting, I took a hit in the chest, and ended up as a POW. How did it happen? Well, a light

German cruiser shelled our vessel, which ripped it apart. What a nightmare, with people running everywhere confused: smoke, fire, explosions, anguish, and pain. Sailors who escaped with no injuries and men who have minor wounds jumped overboard. The Krauts wasted no time coming aboard and taking the rest of us as prisoners. Several shipmates in critical condition died during our transport to Stuttgart, and others perished in camp. I'm one of the lucky ones, that's for sure. We lost some good mates in that battle. I still think about them.

* * *

Lou Ellen

When her husband was off duty, Katerina and the children knew it was family time when the entire day was spent together experiencing new and exciting things. They waded and bathed in the sea, created and destroyed sand castles, strolled along the beach, and gathered interesting shells and stones. At other times, they watched muscular young men dive for coral, or the family strolled through nearby parks and gardens. Many times during those jaunts, Katerina and Pitor marveled at their good fortune and joy. On one occasion, the pair sat quietly on a park bench. When daughter Valentina began fussing, Katerina rocked the baby buggy until she stopped fussing or fell asleep. Meanwhile, as Gregorio took delight in running around the park benches in ever-widening circles, he pleaded with his parents, "Watch me, Momma. See how fast I can run, Poppa." Katerina turned to her husband with a question.

Katerina

"Am I dreaming? I am so unbelievably happy with you and the kids. God is being good to us. Don't you think?"

He agrees. "You are so right, sweetie," he says, laughing and pecking me on the cheek. "Do you remember the day, a long time ago, I promise you that everything will work out for us? Thank the Lord, it finally has."

*　　*　　*

Lou Ellen

On the other hand, in 1951, life rudely disrupted the Brosio family bliss. At the time, Gregorio was four years old, and his sibling Valentina was not quite a year old, when the unimaginable happened, and Katerina's idyllic world suddenly crashed and shattered into pieces.

Katerina

This terrible day begins as every morning does when Pitor leaves the apartment and heads for the base. This particular morning, though, he has an appointment at the base hospital. It is time for his yearly checkup. Just before leaving, he kisses the kids and me. As he opens the door, I still remember the fresh air smell, and seeing the rain pouring down in sheets so hard, Pitor runs back inside and grabs his poncho. "See you later," he hollers. Before he opens the door again, he turns around, smiles, blows kisses our direction, and leaves.

By now, it is close to lunchtime. I am near the window wringing out baby clothes to hang on the rack inside, when I see a navy officer in a white dress uniform coming to my door. Suddenly I think, *Oh, dear God. Something must be very wrong.* Then I see sadness or pain on his face. He looks at the floor and chews his bottom lip. By now, I am anxious and afraid. "Tell me, tell me now," I demand. "What's wrong?" Finally, he chokes it out. "It is your husband, Pitor. I am so sorry to inform you that he suddenly passed away at the hospital while having his medical examination. Please accept my condolences."

My heart feels like it is ready to explode inside my chest. *No, no. This cannot be. You are wrong. Why? I don't understand. This must be a horrible dream*, I am thinking. *My Pitor gone?* The officer helps me up from the chair and asks if I can find someone to watch my kids for a while. My neighbor friend will babysit, I tell him.

Lou Ellen

The officer accompanied Katerina to the hospital and left her with the physician who explained that Pitor died of a massive heart attack on the examination table. "It happened so quickly, Mrs. Brosio, and I am sorry to say all our efforts at resuscitation failed. Please take some comfort in knowing that your dear husband did not suffer. I am so sorry for your loss."

Katerina

I have no money for a funeral or burial, so the military takes care of everything. I will stay only one week at the apartment, even though our rent covers the rest of the month. I explain this to the landlady, also a widow. "*Babcia* (Grandma), I think it's best if I and the kids will leave next week and go to a refugee camp."

"Why do that? You are still good for the several more weeks. I am sorry I cannot refund the money to you. By the way, this is not my decision, it is the property owner's rule."

"Oh, don't think about it," I say. "The kids and I will be just fine."

Lou Ellen

Subsequently, another service member accompanied Katerina to the Polish consulate in Naples, where she presented her husband's death certificate. She also signed documents and papers, which facilitated her move with the children to a refugee camp.

In addition, the military paid Katerina's friend for babysitting the children at her apartment while Katerina prepared for the move. She packed bedding and blankets into a chest, sorted and selected clothing for herself and the children, filled suitcases with her selections, and boxed up a few cooking utensils and other necessities.

Displacement
Camp Bagnoli

Lou Ellen

When Katerina, Gregorio, and Valentina arrived at Camp Bagnoli in 1951, the International Refugee Organization (IRO) operated the camp for displaced persons in Naples, as it had since 1946. The facility, originally built in the 1930s, first housed the Italian War Ministry. Later, the Fascist Youth Organization used the facility for its activities. Subsequently, the German military took possession of the facility and utilized it as an officer candidate school. Furthermore, in the middle of 1940s, the complex became an Italian orphanage until the IRO operated the camp for refugees.

Prior to and during Katerina and her children's stay in the camp, Bagnoli served as a temporary home to as many as ten thousand refugees, most of whom came from Eastern European countries such as Poland, Hungary, Latvia, Romania, and Czechoslovakia, among others. The IRO's primary goal was meeting immediate needs of camp residents by providing basic shelter, food, and health care. Furthermore, the plan was to send them back to their home countries as quickly as possible. However, many displaced persons refused to return to their homelands because the Soviet Union conquered their countries, and they feared reprisal or death if they returned. Although the majority of persons living at Camp Bagnoli no longer had a country or place they called home, they were at various stages of process for emigrating elsewhere. At first, the governments of Canada, Argentina, Brazil, Venezuela, Chile, and Australia allowed Eastern refugees to enter their countries—others did not. Eventually, the United States opened its doors, reluctantly, providing that displaced persons had sponsors who would arrange for housing, employment, and assistance with assimilation.

Katerina

I have all my documents in order because nobody can come here without them. The navy officer hands them over to the camp official, saying, "Katerina has all her papers filled out correctly. She just lost her husband, though, so do not ask her too many questions. Here are her papers." The big doors open, and he goes out. I stay where I am with the kids. In a few minutes, the officer comes back and says the consulate wants me to have a room with a window for the children, if possible. "Is one available?" The answer is yes, so right away, the officer and the sailor carry all our baggage upstairs. When they leave, both men give me a hug and wish us good luck.

All of a sudden, it feels like sadness oozes out of my body. I flop down on a chair and cry hard, carrying on like a starving baby. Four-year-old Gregorio starts bawling too, but baby Valentina is too young to know what is going on. I keep asking myself how can I go on? Will I be able to take care of the children by myself? I still have trouble getting it through my head that Pitor is gone forever and not away at sea. Every night I pray, thanking God I have my two children, and I ask him to make me strong.

*   *   *

Lou Ellen

It was not long before Katerina landed a clerical job working in the rudimentary medical dispensary. Her hours were 3:00 to 11:00 p.m., and her pay was equivalent to one dollar per hour. Because both children turned up their noses at the sight of the standard, gooey-looking cafeteria food, Katerina used a portion of her pay to purchase eggs, bananas, and other food items that vendors sold outside the compound.

A young Czech widow, whose daughter was close to Gregorio's age, volunteered to babysit Gregorio and Valentina while Katerina worked. Katerina reciprocated by letting the widow's daughter stay overnight in Katerina's quarters while the woman labored from 11:00 p.m. to 7:00 a.m. in the cafeteria. Throughout the day, Katerina kept busy cleaning the living area, washing clothing, and keeping her eyes on her own children as well.

Lou Ellen

It was the first time Valentina discovered it was fun running out of her mother's sight until she heard her momma's panicky voice, Katerina remembered. When she was not checking up on her daughter, she admitted she fussed over Gregorio as he dressed for school. The primary school (kindergarten through third grade) was located within the camp.

Meanwhile, a year passed. Katerina and her children were still at their temporary home when a woman down the hall informed Katerina that a nice-looking Romanian man with dark wavy hair had eyes for her. He worked in the kitchen, she added.

Katerina

"I am not kidding," the woman says to me. "I'm serious. While you are in line getting your food, he stares at you, keeps smiling, and acts so taken with you, he cannot keep his eyes on his work. And what do you do? You don't give him the time of day."

Well, why should I? I don't care if he is the king of Siam. I am not interested. A couple of weeks after she tells me this, I do not look at him or pay any attention to him because I want to be by myself with the kids. In the first place, I do not want anybody on my back expecting me to do this or that. Besides, I like things just as they are.

The following week, the man introduces himself as Costi Marku and asks if he can speak with me. I am curious. Why? Before he even opens his mouth, I jump on him. "I am a widow with two little kids," I inform him. "And I absolutely have no time or interest in a boyfriend."

"Okay, okay," he answers half-heartedly. "Good-bye. Forget it."
He walks away in a huff.

Who gives a care?

Lou Ellen

Katerina heard nothing from the Romanian for several weeks
until the same woman who lived down the hall from her announced
that she and Costi chatted recently. She learned he visited the camp
doctor. Costi informed her the doctor was treating burns on his hand
and forearm resulting from his carrying hot food from the oven. She
suggested that Katerina change his bandages and, at the same time,
get to know him. Katerina dismissed her proposal. She does not have
the time.

Katerina

The next day, I am washing clothes and hanging them on the
clotheslines outside the barrack. A couple of us ladies always stick
together on our wash day by taking turns watching that nothing happens to our clothes. You see, these Hungarian women keep stealing
people's wash when it is hanging out to dry. So far, no one can catch
them in the act, and until someone is caught, we will keep watch all
summer.

Anyway, on this day, one of our "clothesline guards" comes to
me and says Costi really would like me to change his bandages. He
explains to her that the dressings get so dirty from working in the
kitchen, he is afraid the burns might become infected. At this point,
I am thinking this man doesn't give up. At the same time, I am wondering what is wrong with helping somebody. Nothing. Still, I am
always on guard, not knowing what will come next. Finally, I give
in, and say to her, "Okay, but tell Costi to wait in the hallway this
afternoon, and I will do it."

Lou Ellen

Late that afternoon, Katerina hauled two pails of hot water
into her living area, preparing for the children's baths. There was
Costi waiting in the hallway. She set down the buckets and invited

him inside. He offered to carry the heavy pails, but she declined. They engaged in small talk while she removed bandages. She proceeded cleaning the injured areas before she applied clean dressings. He commented on her quickness and skill. Katerina replied that she is "an old hand" at that sort of thing from working at hospitals in Berlin and Stuttgart. All the while, she observed him closely.

Katerina

His eyes, like the Baltic Sea, are blue and beautiful. When he talks, they sparkle, reminding me of twinkling stars. His body is nice, stocky, but very strong-looking, with big arms and hands. He is not bad-looking at all; actually, quite handsome. I'll bet my last coin he's a ladies' man, though.

Lou Ellen

Abruptly, Katerina dismissed him, noting that she was happy to help him out but had to get busy with other tasks, such as giving the children their baths before the water cooled off. She pulled out the large galvanized washtub from beneath her bed and poured pails of hot water into it. "Can I fetch more hot water?" he asked. Katerina said she had plenty. As Costi left, he spotted Gregorio. "Hey, Gregorio." He asked, "I like going to the movies here in camp. The next time they show a good one, do you want to go with me?" The five-year-old first looked at his mother, then back again at Costi. "No thank you," he replied in a soft voice.

In the ensuing weeks that melted into months, Katerina gradually warmed up to Costi, but she still learned next to nothing about his past or background. When she quizzed him, Costi admitted, "I really don't have much to tell you"—he looked down at his hands and rubbed them together—"except I am twenty-six years old, and I come from Corabia, Romania, where I was born. I served in the army and ended up fighting along the Western front. Then I went with my comrades to Yugoslavia for more fighting. While I was there, a partisan informed me that both my parents were killed during all the skirmishes and confusion that was rocking Romania. I could not take any more of that, so I threw my weapons down and took off.

Then I worked in a coal mine for a time, bummed my way to Italy, and the authorities accepted me here in Bagnoli. I can never go back to Romania, or I will get…" He pointed his thumb and forefinger at the side of his head.

Katerina

Oh my gosh. When he tells me this, I feel so sorry for him. I know how miserable it is to have no mother or father. I have both parents, but you can hardly call them that. I no can remember their cuddles, hugs, kisses, or even any kind, comforting words.

Lou Ellen

Over time, Katerina warmed up to the Romanian, and the two spent more time with each other and her children. Their friendship grew and matured. Among camp gossipmongers, the scuttlebutt was that the couple were having a torrid affair, which created much curiosity: Is she pregnant? Do her kids like him? Will he move in? Will they marry?

Katerina

Every day, more people get visas and move to countries that will allow immigrants. Word from the grapevine is that Spain, Chile, and Argentina welcome displaced persons. Australia takes thousands of refugees. I hear that the Aussies are happy taking in lots of young women and girls because the country is populated with way more men than women. Canada accepts refugees also. I know several families in camp are excited about going there. These days, so many families and single people are leaving Bagnoli after the announcement is made it will soon close. The camp director says after the place shuts down, the Italian army will house and train their recruits here.

Katerina

Not long afterward, I hear that any single man or woman who has more than one child rarely immigrates to another country. When I hear this, I feel like I am kicked in the stomach by a big Belgian draft horse. I ask the priest for help and wind up running all over

Rome, but nobody can do anything. The embassy people tell me these are the Geneva Convention rules. I cry, moan, and gripe to my friends. A big Italian momma who married a Russian hears my goings-on and takes me aside. "Listen, honey," she says in such a soft voice that I can hardly hear her, "there is still hope for you. All you have to do is marry your handsome Romanian. Then you can leave this place and go to any country you like. Listen to me. If life is no good with him, all you have to do is divorce him and start over again with another man. There are plenty of fish in the sea yet." I thank her for the advice and say I will think about it.

Finally, the news comes from our camp director. It turns out that our new home is another displacement—or waiting camp—as I call it, in nearby Salerno. We have only one week to pack up our belongings. How will I manage? It dawns on me. I will ask this love-sick Romanian.

Later, Costi and I have a long talk. For him, going back to Romania is out of the question. The people in power do so many flip-flops, he says, the government could accuse him of going AWOL (absent without leave) or worse. He doesn't want the chance spending time in prison or being shot for cooperating with the enemy. I have no desire to return to my country, either. Poland is nothing but a faraway memory full of sadness, abuse, and misery. Only a nutcase will even consider this. Right now, Poland is under communist control.

Costi and I agree on one thing: good friends stick together no matter what. This describes us. We are just friends, but are we lovers? Heck no. I am twenty-eight years old and still young. Besides, I like living by myself with Gregorio and Valentina. I do not want a guy hanging on my back. I cook, eat, sleep, and play with the kids whenever I want. I do not need a man telling me to do this and do that.

Finally, the day arrives when all of us refugees leave Camp Bagnoli and move once again to another temporary home named Mercatello.

Mercatello

Lou Ellen

The refugee camp was located along the southern Italian coast in the Umbia region, near a small town named Mercatello. When Katerina and her fellow Banoli refugees arrived there in 1951, the compound housed five hundred to one thousand persons. The numbers varied because camps closed as refugees left and sought new lives in various countries. Persons still waiting for permission to emigrate were constantly transferred to other displacement camps still operated by the International Refugee Organization.

Katerina

The good part about being here is that we have more space and a bit more privacy. People with kids receive housing in metal Quonset shelters. Each family lives in the hut side by side. Costi also resides in the same kind of dwelling with three other single men. My being here is nice for the kids because the weather is very warm and sunny almost year around. They too can play outdoors even in the coldest months of January and February, when the temperature reaches ten degrees centigrade (fifty degrees Fahrenheit). Living close to the sea has another advantage. The kids love playing in the water or exploring along the shore. My little Italians never tire of pestering me with "Please, Momma. Can we go to the seashore today?"

What I do not like about camp life is having people under your nose all the time and listening to their constant complaining, arguing, and gossiping. The worst part is not having enough food. We are always hungry. The food we wind up getting is not that good anyway. No wonder we have so much sickness around here. Another bad part about refugee life is wondering what happens next. The only thing you can count on is change. Every person here knows this is the truth. So far, all the camps I have been in are pretty much the same, and the people running them try doing their best. Conditions could be much worse, so I do not like to…excuse me, but bitch and moan like a wicked witch.

Lou Ellen

Mercatello officials regularly stressed how important it was for refugees to learn new skills, which could prove helpful for émigrés finding jobs in their new homelands. Therefore, residents are encouraged to choose among various offerings such as sewing, cooking, food preservation, farming skills, carpentry, shoe repair, and learning foreign languages, among other practical courses.

Katerina

Costi takes up carpentry and painting classes, and in the workshop, he meets a Czech man with missing one hand. I can speak very good with him. Polish and Czech languages are much the same. He plans on going to Chicago in the USA, where he says a relative will sponsor him. I am curious about his missing hand, so I ask for details. He explains that he no longer moves fast enough when ordered, so a half-crazy German guard whacked four fingers off one hand but left a thumb, and he darn near bled to death. Just when I am anxious to hear the rest, Costi cuts in and says he has something for me. He does not tell me what but takes me aside after supper and says, "I think we should get married."

"Why now?" I want to know.

"For the kids," he answers. "Together, we will be one family, leave here together, and go to Australia, Spain, France, or anywhere else you want. We will make a good home. Think about it."

I ask him if this is his surprise. He kisses both my cheeks and says, "No, not exactly. I have a real surprise. I have something to give you, but you must wait until your birthday. Be patient."

Well, after I keep hounding Costi's missing-finger-friend to finish his story, he says after the guard cut off his fingers, they left him lying on the floor, screaming in pain while the SS man slinked away, carefree and calm. His fellow bunkmates did their best stopping the bleeding and bandaging his stumps, but infection set in, then gangrene. After the Czech's fingers turned black, he says he wound up in the hospital where a surgeon amputated his hand at the wrist.

*　　*　　*

Lou Ellen

Many nights thereafter, Katerina lay awake thinking over Costi's proposal, and she prayed for divine guidance. In addition, she realized the importance of giving Gregorio and Valentina a father, a permanent home, and a new, good life. She decided she would not make a decision until she spent time mulling over all the pros and cons she could think of.

Meanwhile, the camp administrator received word that Katrina was proficient in Polish, German, Czech, and Romanian languages, and that she was reputed to be an excellent translator. Consequently, he hired her to assist fellow refugees with completing their emigration paperwork.

Katrina

Before anybody can emigrate, there are many forms to fill out. Then you have to get all these different people to sign them: Italian and American doctors, American officers, consulate officials, and others. All this drags on and on. Sometimes, you wait months before your quota number comes up. I have the visas for the children and me, but we wait like everybody else.

Lou Ellen

In the interim, Costi accepted a position as camp police officer. His duties included helping resolve disputes among residents, making security rounds at night, and assisting the police captain track down and round up runaways.

In May, the week of Katerina's birthday, Costi sprang his surprise—a wood-burning cookstove, complete with an oven that his one-hand Czech friend designed and fabricated.

Katerina

My, oh my. I cannot believe my good fortune. My new stove has a nice oven for baking, and two flat round areas on top for cooking. This stove is just what I need since I no can eat much camp food. The kitchen only uses lard in their cooking, and the doctor believes this is making me sick. Anyway, many women here are jealous because I am the only person in Mercatello who owns a cookstove. A jealous lady always complains to the police captain and asks him, "Why is she so special, huh?" He explains that it is my private stove and suggests, "If you want one similar, go to town and buy one." Well, she never acts on his recommendation, but continues her complaining. Actually, I doubt if there exists another stove like mine anywhere around.

It's not that I am stingy, either. I do use the stove to help others when I cook for sick residents; otherwise, I offer the use of my stove to any woman or man who wants to cook a special meal for an ailing family member and others who fancy baking sweet treats for spouses or children on their birthdays and other special occasions. Really, I adore everything about my birthday gift, and I love Costi for his kindness and generosity to my kids and myself. I hug and kiss him and let him know how much I love and respect him. When I do this, he always perks up and shines. Then one evening, his mood turns cloudy. For a minute, he hems and haws around. Finally, he blurts out that he has something important to tell me, something I should know. Suddenly, my stomach turns a flip-flop. After he stalls around for what seems like forever, Costi finally lets the bomb drop. It blows me away. Prior to the war, he confesses that he married a hometown girl. During his army service in Germany, Yugoslavia, and beyond, he heard no word from her.

Lou Ellen

Costi then tried contacting her—without success. When the war ended, and he was living at the displacement camp in Bagnoli, he checked on his wife's whereabouts. From friends in his hometown, Costi learned his wife died from pneumonia. He also discovered he fathered a little girl, which his late wife's relatives were raising.

Katerina

I am shocked and heartbroken. I bawl like a colicky baby, and I feel like throwing up. "Are you serious?" He nods. "Are you telling me that you have a wife and a child this whole time, and you never tell me the truth until now? For crying out loud, you make me sick to my stomach. Do you know that? Listen. This child of yours, Costi. What will you do with her, huh?"

"I don't have answers to any of your questions," Costi answers. "But give me time. All I know for sure is that I love you, and I am very sorry I hurt you. I will work everything out. You will see. Just trust me. Can you can do that?"

Lou Ellen

The more Katerina thought about his dilemma, the more she understood his reluctance for revealing details of his past for fear of losing her. She admitted to me that if she knew about his wife and child when she first met him, she would have lost her temper, told him to get lost, and never bother her or her kids ever again.

Nevertheless, during the following months, Katerina and Costi gradually ironed out their personal difficulties, which drew them closer together. Costi's most troublesome predicament was what to do with his daughter. Katerina reminded him that he could do nothing until he immigrated to a permanent home, found a job, and settled down—all of which might take years.

Katerina

I also remind my boyfriend that he cannot take his daughter away from the relatives raising her. By now, they are the only momma and poppa she knows. On the other hand, I suggest that if we marry and settle down to a new life in a new country, we can always invite her to visit us when she grows up and makes her own decisions. "Maybe she can even come and live with us," I say.

*   *   *

Lou Ellen

Meanwhile, Katerina mulled over the pros and cons of marrying Costi. He was a good worker; he loved her and the kids and was kind and thoughtful. On the other hand, he did not reveal much about his past; he had a vague family background, and he frequently let his temper blow. However, the fact that she did not experience the same deep feeling of love and contentment with Costi as she had with her first husband troubled her. The twinge of conscience she felt left her uncertain. She tried ignoring it, she confessed to me, but kept dithering. She prayed and prayed again, asking for direction. Finally, she had an answer. Still, she was not certain she was choosing her heart over mind in the matter. Which was most important?

Katerina

I decide I will give Costi my consent for marriage, but I will not mention that I am having a royal battle between my heart and mind. Truthfully, I do not want marriage at this time, but I ask myself what action I can take that will bring out the best for my children. Before long, they will begin a new life in a strange country. The answer is clear: a father. When I give my decision to Costi, we will let his boss, the police captain, know we want to marry as soon as possible.

Lou Ellen

The captain informed Katerina's future spouse that two other couples in the camp also desired matrimony. Once everyone's proper paperwork was completed, he said, he would contact authorities at the town hall in Mercatello's city center and arrange a date for all the couples repeating their vows the same day.

*   *   *

Katerina

Finally, after several weeks of filling out papers and rounding up documents that show proof we are fit for a civil marriage, the captain takes us to the town hall. Here we are, waiting for the mayor. At last, the chamber door opens. He gives a short talk in Italian to one couple at a time, vows are said, and within twenty minutes, the simple civil ceremony is over. Each new husband and wife acts as a witness to another couple. After saying our vows, the mayor says, "I now present to everyone the new Mr. and Mrs. Marku." Now my kids have a father, and we are husband and wife for better or worse.

Not one of us has on fancy clothes, but I wear a clean dress with an imitation red rose pinned below my left shoulder. Costi wears dark trousers and a white shirt he borrows from a fellow refugee.

Lou Ellen

Back at camp, there was no celebrating, according to Katerina. There was no music, dancing, special food, or gifts. Each newly married couple went his own way, and life went on as usual. The new husbands were the exception. They kept busy moving their meager belongings from single male housing to family quarters.

*   *   *

The first year of Katerina and Costi's married life inched ahead; to them, seemingly slower than a slimy crawling slug. Month after month dragged on, while the couple and the children waited to depart. Meanwhile, everyone around them, families and individuals, were leaving for new beginnings in Canada, England, Australia, Chile, Brazil, and Argentina, among other countries.

Katerina

While we wait for Mercatello's closing, my husband and I haven't decided which country that accepts refugees we should choose to begin our new lives. Already, a few neighbors try talking us into selecting Spain because it is where they are going. I guess they want company, and I understand why. It is much easier adjusting to drastic change when someone you know is going through the same experience. Also, these folks believe that I know nearly every language (which I don't) and say how nice it is speaking and understanding a strange country's native tongue. I hate admitting this, but I do not like any part of Spain or its language. The fast, garbled speech sounds weird, and it's hard for me understanding what people say.

At this time, I guess all we can do is wait patiently and wonder what the holdup is. In the meantime, every week I study the emigration list in the office. It gives the last names of people who are leaving. At first, I do not understand the meaning of the word pending, which is always written at the end of our last name. After all these months of waiting and watching, I wonder if the *not yet* word will ever disappear from the list. It is hard to believe that something like this takes so much time.

Lou Ellen

Subsequently, Katerina and her two children had their visas in order, as did Costi. The couple selected America as their new home country. Nearly everyone at Mercatello believed that the United States was the best country in the entire world. However, when their interviews with various emigration officials were completed, and all papers signed and documents gathered, the family was finally prepared to leave camp and begin a new life. Suddenly, there was a major glitch.

Katerina

Talk about unlucky! This news could not come at a worse time. We are blowing our chance to start life in America, and at this moment, I am upset and disappointed. When I spring the news on Costi, he is thrilled I am pregnant. He hugs and kisses me on both cheeks and pats my belly. "This will be our first baby together," he says, laughing. "But I want two or three more." For heaven's sake, is he out of his mind? We already have two children. Does he forget them? My husband doesn't see me jumping up and down with joy over the news. My pregnancy means we must wait here again until the baby is born. How depressing! Will we ever lay our eyes on America? On the other hand, I believe babies are one of our Maker's miracles. For this I am thankful. After all, everything works out for the best, doesn't it? Now we need patience. Then we will wait and see what happens next.

Lou Ellen

Later, adding to the family's upheaval, is Costi's unwelcome report that the refugee camp at Mercatello will close. Thus, current residents will relocate to another DP camp in nearby Salerno.

Katerina

At first, I do not believe him. Not again! "Who tells you this?" I ask my husband. "A poor peasant off the street? Your boss in security? You must be joking. Oh my gosh."

*   *   *

Lou Ellen

In 1953, the nine-month wait for the Marku family finally ended. Katerina gave birth to a healthy baby girl at a civilian hospital in Salerno. Since the closing of Mercatello was delayed, the Marku family continued living at Mercatello with the remaining displaced persons.

Katerina

Costi and I name our little darling Rosa. She is pretty as a pink rosebud, and she has my husband's dark hair. She is hungry all the time, as he is too. I feed her by breast every two hours and sometimes more. We are so proud and happy with this child; she is so easy to care for. When Rosa is nearly two months old, this camp finally closes, which means we must pack up and move again. Hopefully, it is our last stop.

Camp Salerno

Lou Ellen

Traveling to Salerno, Katerina and her family were among the five hundred remaining displaced persons jammed into the back of open military trucks like baby dill pickles crammed into jars. A long line of trucks preceded their vehicle, each of which contained a jumble of family belongings and essential goods such as bedding and blankets, clothing, cooking utensils, baby items, and a few simple toys. As soon as the lurching truck stopped in the compound's parking area, all conversation halted. Jaws dropped in disbelief. Nearly every DP stared at the twelve-foot-high wire fence topped with curly concertina wire that surrounded the entire complex.

Katerina

I cannot believe my eyes. Are we in prison here? I ask this of the truck driver who jumps out and comes around to help us out to the ground. "No, no, no," he says in a booming voice. "Mussolini used this spot to keep out-of-control bad boys who steal, fight, and kill. After the partisans kill Mussolini and the war ends, the Allies take this place over and fix it nice for you refugees. You will like it here." I say to my husband I will thank God for this. He should too.

Lou Ellen

As was the case with most passengers, Katerina, Costi, and the children were hot, sweaty, and tired. After cramps were massaged out, legs stretched, and wandering children were reigned in, the family was directed to a long wooden barrack. It was situated among rows and rows of similar structures. Each building, divided into twelve rooms, had three corridors, which led to four living areas. Since Katerina and Costi had three children, the family was allocated two and a half rooms. Within a short time, both Katerina and Costi landed paid jobs. Once again, Katerina served as a translator, assisting individuals as they filled out immigration papers. She assisted them by clarifying words and phrases in several languages in which she was fluent.

Costi's experience as a security officer enabled him to start working immediately on the night shift. He assisted the police captain with peacekeeping duties among various ethnic groups, helped investigate and solve petty thefts, and aided officials conducting background checks on suspicious persons, among other duties.

Katerina

Life is good here for most people, and much better for those who have jobs like my husband and me. We are in good with the camp director, police captain, and the visiting priest, which gives us few extra benefits. Office workers ask if I will take on an extra job sorting piles of clothes that churches in America and other groups send us. People can select what they need every month on what is called Monday Clothing Day. Sure, I'll be happy to help, I say. Now I have the privilege of choosing clothes for the kids, my husband, and myself before other women pick them over.

A neighbor lady, who sometimes watches my kids, helps me sort through the piles. We choose large-size good dresses and take them back to the barrack. She is a very good seamstress. Together, we cut and sew, then wash and iron the clothing we make over. Once we finish our work, my daughters always wind up with very nice dresses. We do the same with the men's and boys' outfits, which give Costi and Gregorio nice shirts, trousers, and jackets. The room where they keep the clothing is next to the chapel, so on what we call Pick and Pitch day, the two of us sit outside the door while other female refugees come inside and make their selections. When the women come out with their choices, my friend and I write down their names, number of kids they have, and how many pieces they take. The camp manager keeps these records on file in the office.

Lou Ellen

In addition to Katerina's sorting duties and translating position, for which she receives a small amount of pay, she volunteers to set up the altar for both Protestant and Catholic services.

Katerina

I take a clean altar cloth and put it in place. Then I always arrange the flowers I pick outdoors on extra tables, so the chapel looks pretty when people come in and pray. Every time I do this, I find the same young man sitting on the chapel steps. "Hello," he says, grinning. Then he follows me inside and keeps talking. "Lady, you have kids and still you work here, there, and everywhere. How many places can one woman work, anyway?"

"I can work as long as I am alive and kicking," I explain.

"Yeah, I can tell. And your kids always look nice and clean too."

Yah, I do my best to keep my husband and kids halfway decent-looking. I must be doing something right because the refugee commissioner from Switzerland comes quite often, checking up on how well the camp is being run. He always stops at our barrack and asks if he may come inside and check out our rooms.

Lou Ellen

Katerina described the commissioner's frequent, unexpected visits irritating. Later, she asked the camp director why he always selected the Marku place for inspection. The director explained, "Simple. Your three children are always polite, look well-dressed and clean. Besides that, the kitchen area in back is always trim and tidy. You wash your pots and pans, turn them upside down to dry. All the boots and shoes line up in a row, and your firewood is even stacked neatly beside the stove. Every room is spotless, with not even a hint of clutter anywhere. Gee, Katerina, how can I not bring the commissioner to your place?"

The family quickly settled into their new dwelling, and life at Salerno went on as usual. Eight-year-old Gregorio hopped on a 7:00 a.m. bus that ferried him to school close by the center. According to Katerina, he loved school and was an excellent student. He also received his first communion at Pompeii and, afterward, became an altar boy for the visiting priest who offered weekly mass at the camp.

Valentina who was four years old attended preschool classes, also held within the compound. She enjoyed playing with her classmates and loved to sing, sway, and clap her hands along with the music.

Conversely, one-year-old Rosa caused her mother much anxiety and concern. During the baby's routine exam at the dispensary, Katerina informed the doctor that Rosa did not act right.

Katerina

"Explain further," he says to me. "Describe to me her behavior."

"Well," I say, "for instance, Rosa has no appetite like before, and she spends more time sleeping. And look. My baby's nice rosy cheeks are gone. Tell me, Doctor. What is wrong with her?"

Lou Ellen

However, having a sickly child was not Katerina's only concern. Another matter weighed heavily on her mind, and it involved her husband Costi.

Katerina

Believe me, I am telling the truth. Well, one day a while back, I go to the dentist. He makes me a new set of upper teeth. My real ones are a sorry-looking sight. Most are rotten because they half-starved us at Dachau. Anyway, I come home and see that my suitcase lock is broken, and baby Rosa is on the floor playing with cut-up photos. They are in pieces, scattered all over the floor. Right away, I know that these are pictures of my first husband, Pitor. I always keep them in what I believe is a very safe place—hiding them between my clothes and linens near the bottom of the case. I keep them for Gregorio and Valentina. When they grow up, I can imagine them begging like this: "Oh, please, Momma, tell us stories about our real poppa. What does he look like? Do you have pictures? We want to see. Do we have his nose, his eyes, or the color of his hair?"

All at once, I scream, yell, and cry at Costi. "Why do you do this? I cannot understand you at all. I cannot believe you are so mean and cruel. I hate you. Get out of my sight and do not speak to me, again. Do you hear me?"

"Listen," he says in an ice-cold voice. "I don't have any photographs of my family. Why should you have pictures of this son of a bitch."

Is this the man I marry? He doesn't give a rat's hind end for my feelings. Over the next few days, I never bawl so much in my whole life. I am so upset, I give him the cold shoulder and silent treatment for days on end. I will give him a dose of his own medicine. It serves him right. I hope that he will wake up.

Finally, days later, he apologizes for his meanness and jealousy, and he begs me to forgive him. He cries and says he cannot figure out why he acts this way. I wonder too. Is it because he comes from a war zone or fights on the front? Maybe he is still grieving over dead parents. Who knows the answer?

Eventually, I give in. Many days later, I admit to Costi that I am no perfect angel, either, and I forgive him. We hug, kiss, go to bed, and make up. Still, I carry a heavy heart.

Lou Ellen

Several weeks passed before Katerina conjured up enough courage to inform her contrite husband of another problem. She announced that she was pregnant again with their fourth child. Katerina was surprised that he was pleased. He pecked her on the cheek, patted her belly, and proudly said, "Oh, good, Momma. Do you remember? Before we marry, I tell you that I want many kids. I still do."

Katerina

Yah, yah. I do remember, but I remind Costi that me being with baby again shuts the door on our immigration until this child is born. He comes back with, "Why didn't you think about this, first?"

"Me? What about you? You're the one who makes the excuse for not using birth control because you say we don't have enough money to buy these stupid things." I think to myself, *Use your brain, Costi. Raising another child also takes money.*

*　　*　　*

Lou Ellen

Added to the couple's mounting concern was baby Rosa's illness. The camp physician informed them that he could not pinpoint a medical diagnosis, but he would do everything in his power to help their child. However, Katerina believed that her beautiful little girl with curly dark hair appeared much sicker than before.

She was often feverish and cried more often than usual, Katerina explained, and she had bouts of vomiting and diarrhea.

In the ensuing weeks, the physician continued giving Rosa vitamins and antibiotics. He also suggested Katerina feed her a bland diet. He promised he would do everything in his power identifying the baby's problem and treating her until she regained good health. His goal, he said, was accomplishing this before the family immigrated. He also stated he was confident everything would work out for the family, but on the slim chance something unexpected happened, he had a suggestion she and her husband should consider.

Katerina

The doctor wants Costi and me to think about giving Rosa up to him and his wife. I never forget his words: "If your baby is not well by the time you immigrate to your new home, my wife and I will love her, raise her, and treat her as our own. My wife cannot have children, and you and your husband have good recommendations from everyone in camp. She is such a beautiful child, and we will consider it a privilege to have her."

After Costi and I talk this over, I tell the doctor that we cannot give her up. Rosa is our child. I thank the doctor for his kindness and doing all he can to help her, but I tell him I will put her health and everything else in God's hands. This is all I can do.

*　　*　　*

Lou Ellen

In 1955, Katerina gave birth to a son who was born at a civilian hospital in nearby Naples. The baby, named Gabi, and his youngest sibling, Rosa, were fifteen months apart in age.

Katerina

My husband is so proud of his firstborn son we choose for him a Romanian name. Gabi means hero of God. Soon after the baby comes, I begin coughing. It lasts nearly a week. My muscles ache too, and I am tired all the time. Some days I am so cold, I cannot seem to warm up, and then I am hot and sweaty. Costi insists I go to the dispensary and have the doctor examine me. After he checks my X-rays, the doctor says I have double pneumonia, which I guess is worse than the regular kind. "Double pneumonia means there is infection in both of your lungs," he explains. "The disease is usually caused by bacteria or a virus. If this type of pneumonia is untreated, serious complications can develop. It's a good thing you came in to see me, Mrs. Marku."

Now I am popping pills, drinking lots of water, and trying to follow the doctor's order that I get plenty of rest. Until I feel better, a pleasant young Latvian woman who lives in the barrack across from us suggests she take on our family wash. She even offers to help with daily chores.

She is such a nice, kind person, but a few nasty people here push her around. After I recuperate and am back to my old self again, I watch while she tries moving away from a man who is bothering her outside the barrack. All at once, I notice he grabs her arm, pulls her around facing her, and shoves. I rush over and ask if he has a brain. "Of course," he snorts.

"What in the world did she ever do to you?" I ask.

"Nothing," he mumbles under his breath.

Well, by this time, I am so mad, I hit him on the chest as hard as I can. He goes "Ahh." Next, I chew his butt out good, call him a few nasty names, and give him a piece of my mind. "There, how does that feel?"

He doesn't answer but flashes a nasty sneer. I yell back at him that now he knows exactly what it feels like, right?

All at once, the Latvian woman breaks out bawling because she is either embarrassed or ashamed; I do not know which. In either case, this type of scabby treatment happens anywhere, not only in DP camps. Just because people are kind and quiet, dirt bags are always around ready to pounce on them. You absolutely cannot allow anyone stepping all over you. If you do, the bully will keep stomping harder. This is my theory, anyway, which is based on my experience. Don't get me wrong. Most people are good, generous, and kind. The few rotting apples in the world are the ones who taste the most bitter in my mouth.

*   *   *

Lou Ellen

Following Gabi's birth, Katerina and Costi reapplied for immigration, a procedure that often involved months and, sometimes, years for completion. The remaining five hundred residents at Camp Salerno, whose homelands included Eastern European countries such as Poland, Latvia, Lithuania, Yugoslavia, and Czechoslovakia, among others, had two options: One dealt with facing the uncertainty of a new and strange life in a democratic society. The other choice was facing the reality of death or exile by returning to their former home countries. At that period, most of those countries were in the hands of the Soviet Union communists or their puppet regimes.

Katerina

People operating the camp tells us great things about Australia and say we should go there. Right away, my husband and I ignore their suggestion. We have our hearts set on living in America, the country everyone says is the best in the world. Every time I visit the consulate, I remind the officials I will help with translation or work at anything free, so long as our family goes to America. I care less about living anywhere else.

Lou Ellen

As was the case with all refugees planning immigration, Katerina, Costi, and their four children were required to undergo physical and mental health examinations and receive a series of vaccinations, which guarded against various diseases. The preliminary action required filling out many forms and acquiring signatures from both Italian and American physicians. There were also interrogations and interviews with American political inspectors and consular officials. In addition, the couple needed to apply and receive new visas. Since Katerina's home country was Poland, she was not allowed entrance into the United States until her quota number came up.

The quota was the result of the US Congress having passed the Immigration and Nationality Provision of 1952, also known as the McLaren-Walter Act, which admitted into the United States a certain number of refugees based on nationality. Some opponents of the United States viewed the act as discrimination. Proponents, however, believed the provision protected the United States from infiltration by communists, which they believed were a serious threat to America's security and welfare.

In the spring of 1959, five years had passed since Katerina and her family first arrived at Camp Salerno. In that year, however, their names on the emigration status sheet changed from "pending" to "active." The couple's dream for a new home and a new life appeared certain.

Katerina

I thank God he answers my prayers. Rosa, now five years old, is over her sickness. She goes to camp school and is a happy child. These days, we sit at the dinner table, talk about America, and describe our new lives. My husband believes we will live like kings.

Gregorio, twelve, imagines us having lots of money, and he thinks he will be famous someday. You are all dreaming, I say, laughing. Yes, sir! We will make good in America, I point out, but only if we work very hard. Never forget this.

A few days later, I just come home from the office after working three hours translating. Well, as soon as I open the door, Gregorio meets me there, jumping up and down, and waving his arms real excited. "Mom," he yells, "you have a letter. It looks important."

"Sweetheart," I say, "is it open?"

My son shakes his head. He reminds me that he does not open envelope letters unless they are for him. I praise him and give him permission to open it. He opens the letter, looks it over quickly, and makes a face. "Hurry up," I urge, "and read it."

"Mom," he says, groaning, "it's all in English." I ask him to read it, anyway. I want to know how much English he is learning in school. He rereads the letter, this time more slowly. He finishes, then jumps up and down like his shoes are fastened with springs and bursts out shouting in Italian, *"Mamma, stiamo andando verso gli Sati Uniti!"* (Mom, we are going to the United States!)

Lou Ellen

The following day, the family celebrated their good news. Katrina bartered with a local farmer who offered a live hen in exchange for a loaf of her bread and a flannel shirt that Costi no longer wanted.

Katerina

Farmer Filberto is so happy to have my homemade bread and the shirt, he gives me a bag filled with apples. In the camp, fruit is scarce as hen's teeth, as they say. Afterward, Costi kills the chicken for me while I boil the water. Next, I hold the hen by its feet and swish it up and down in the bubbling steamy water. The feathers are still on the bird, which makes it easier to dress. The first step is gutting the hen. Then I pluck the feathers. All that is left of the feathers are the tiny pinfeathers I singe off with a burning candle. The bird is nearly ready for the oven, but first, I rinse it off and stuff it with chopped apple and stale bread pieces. Finally, I slide it into the oven. I no more close the oven door when Grandma, a Polish woman across the hall, comes and knocks on the door. She needs to use my oven right away, she explains. "I'm sorry," I say, "but you can't use it right now. My family's supper is in there, baking. It will not be ready for at least an hour."

"Oh my goodness," she says, pulling a long face. "My bread needs baking right away. What will I do?" She acts so gloomy I open the oven and scoot a few pans around until there is more room on the top rack. Still, it looks like a tight fit. After I push my potatoes into an empty corner space, I show Grandma where she can place her cake. "Fan-tas-tic!" she cries out. To this day, I still picture happiness bubbling over her face.

Grandma's bread recipe is traditional Polish, which most people bake during Easter. The dough is fashioned into a sixteen-inch long loaf with sausage and eggs. The raw eggs, still inside the shell, are inserted in the dough at three-inch intervals. When her bread finishes cooling, Grandma leaves us half a loaf. Gregorio warns everyone not to eat her bread. "The eggs inside the bread are still in their shells," he explains, wrinkling his nose. "You will choke to death on the shells if you swallow them."

I explain. "Listen, sweetie. First, cut a thick slice. Then remove the egg, still in its shell. Crack it, pick it clean, and enjoy a tasty hard-boiled egg along with your bread. It's so simple."

"But, Mom," he argues. "I am scared to eat it because I don't want to get appendicitis."

Again, I explain there is no danger. Finally, he understands and eats a small piece. Then he runs outdoors.

When it is time to eat supper, I call the kids inside. Everyone sits at the table, and there is no fighting or fooling around. Costi is very strict with the kids too and insists that they behave properly. After we finish eating, the kids stack all our dishes in the corner, and I rinse them with cold water. If you do not rinse dishes right away, it is so hot and dry in Italy, food sticks on the plates, knives, forks, and other stuff. Then it is hard to scrape off. When all the dishes, pots, utensils, and tableware is clean and has the final rinse, I let them air dry. It is Gregorio's job to put everything back in its usual place.

After supper, Costi usually takes a nap before he works security at night. The kids know they cannot cut up or holler when their father is trying to sleep. Sometimes they forget, but they know exactly what comes next. This is the time when Costi whips out the leather razor strop and whacks their rear ends.

*   *   *

In the morning, my husband tells me that some Yugoslav communists are in camp, and security is looking for them. They nab one man in Naples. It is no surprise. I am very suspicious of a few characters hanging around in Camp Salerno. These men are not friendly, and they mostly keep to themselves. The short scraggly guy roams all around the grounds taking photos. He is the one I translate immigration paper for a while back. Maybe something doesn't check out, but it seems everybody has some sort of problem. Right now, my concern is helping my kids and husband prepare for a new life in the United States of America. All the time, I hear America is the land of milk and honey where the streets are paved with gold. People believe this. If you ask me, anyone spouting this nonsense is one brick short of a full load, or whatever. Anyhow, I am sick and tired from constantly waiting and moving, and I can hardly stomach the thought of another temporary displacement camp that often turns into a years-on-end camp. As you can imagine, my patience is fading.

*   *   *

Lou Ellen

The day the Marku family looked forward to for years arrived. They finally overcame the many obstacles that faced all refugees seeking immigration to other countries. The largest hurdle for Katrina's family was obtaining an American entrance visa that was required for booking passage on a ship. Then, in addition, she and her husband had to acquire a waiting quota number established for their countries of birth. Other requirements included affidavits of support and sponsorship and proof of good health from the US consulate in Italy.

With all the bureaucracy and paperwork behind them, the family could immigrate. The year was 1959. At that time, Gregorio was a fourteen-year-old teenager, followed by nine-year-old Valentina, six-year-old Rosa, and Gabi, who was four. Packing for the voyage began immediately.

Katerina

I sort and pack the children's clothes and a few toys first. Costi's belongings come next. He is so persnickety about how he wants his shirts, trousers, and underwear placed in the suitcase, it drives me nuts. Other than taking along my clothing and a few personal items, I am also taking sugar, flour, and a few enamel pots and pans. I have no idea whether these things are available in America. After all, I have no money to buy whatever the family needs, anyway.

All the time I am pushing and pressing our belongings into boxes and suitcases, I debate whether I should tell anyone about my suspicion—not even my husband. Revealing my secret could again delay our leaving for the United States. Just the thought makes me miserable.

I believe I am again with baby, but I am not positive. I did miss my period this month though. The consulate doctor who gives me the final health check announces, "You are good to go, Katerina, at last." Maybe he knows but keeps quiet. Is it a blessing or luck?

* * *

Lou Ellen

Immigration officials notified Katerina and Costi that the Peaceful Valley Church in Milltown was acting as their sponsor. The couple learned Milltown was a small city located in the midwest section of the United States. They also understood that the church provided their housing, assisted them in seeking jobs, and was willing to help them in any way possible.

With everything packed and everyone ready to go, the Marku family climbed aboard the International Refugee Organization (IRO) truck that transported refugees to Naples. The IRO, affiliated with the United Nations, was the same group that operated Camp Salerno.

America Bound

Lou Ellen

At Naples, Katerina recalled, the family lived in a barrack for a few days while repairs were completed on the vessel that would transport its passengers to the United States. Despite another delay, Katerina described her fellow refugees as patient, understanding, and excited.

Katerina

People in charge put mothers and kids in one section of the barrack and men in another. There is no kitchen available, so they give us money to buy food. I cannot tell my husband about me with baby. He will not be happy, I am sure. Besides, if I tell him now, he will probably blab to all the men and ship officials, and they might send us back to another DP camp until I give birth.

Lou Ellen

The vessel Katerina and her family would board for the transatlantic voyage was the 630-foot-long Saturnia, built in 1927. At that time, the ship operated passenger and cargo service. During the war, the US Army Transport Service commandeered the ship, and its name became the Frances Y. Slanger. During the war, it served as a hospital troop ship. However, in 1947, the United States returned the vessel to the Italian line, and she reclaimed her original name.

On May 18, 1959, the vessel, with its propeller repaired, left the harbor. It sailed out to the Tyrrhenian Sea, heading for Mediterranean waters with Katerina and her family aboard. They joined an additional 400 to 550 passengers, all of whom were refugees. The largest group among them was Poles and Lithuanians. The remainder included Ukrainians, Hungarians, Yugoslavians, Romanians, among a few others.

Katerina

Oh my. We are crammed together on this boat like little fishes in a shiny tin. Nowhere on this ship can a person spend time alone. Sleeping quarters for mommas and their squalling kids are in one section of the ship. Men and boys bunk in the opposite end, which is a long walk away. Costi has Gregorio with him, and the other four kids are with me. Most afternoons, families come together on the main deck and talk about the things we hear about America: nobody is poor, there are plenty of jobs, and there is no such thing as being hungry. Some people believe Americans cover their streets with gold, and if you live in America, you know heaven. Really? I wonder how much is true or if their talk is just a bunch of ballyhoo.

Lou Ellen

Once the Saturnia entered the Mediterranean Sea, Katerina said, the balmy weather suddenly changed. A chill wind blew in and gradually intensified. The vessel listed. Bright blue water churned, curled, and spit into a frothy, mousey gray. Many passengers scampered for refuge below deck. Others appeared fascinated by Mother Nature's power. Most of those daring souls wound up running to the nearest railing where they heaved and spewed vomit overboard. Many older adults and children failed at making it to the ship's railing on time, and before long, a sickening stench wafted throughout the ship.

In the dining area, dishes slid and slithered across tables then shattered into pieces. Chairs tipped and tumbled along the floor.

Katerina

I am sick since we leave Naples's harbor. Now during this stormy weather, I am throwing up like a volcano. Costi believes I am hit bad with seasickness. I do not tell him about our baby number five. If I do, he will cuss, yell, and use all kinds of nasty words in his anger. This is not good for the children. I will tell him about the baby when the time is right.

Lou Ellen

The next few days were calm. Seasickness among passengers subsided. Adults and older children kept their sleeping areas clean and tidy. Females, both single and married, helped with dishes, and others cleaned the dining area, while able-bodied men and older boys assisted the crew painting decks or working in the engine room. Ship staff members made daily reports regarding the number of nautical miles the ocean liner completed during the previous twenty-four hours. The first mate announced that the entire crossing would cover more than four thousand nautical miles.

Saturnia made her first stop at the Strait of Gibraltar, a channel that connected the Mediterranean Sea to the Atlantic Ocean. The crew off-loaded cargo and took additional passengers aboard. Passengers from Naples go ashore for a short period; they stretched their sea legs and took the opportunity to buy fruit and other goodies from dockside vendors.

Katerina

Costi and our older kids cannot wait to get off the ship. They have money the priest at Salerno gives us the day before we leave Italy. Holy Father gives the kids and me his blessing because we are Catholic. "Costi is Orthodox and is at work," I tell Father.

He says, "I do not want to leave your husband out because it is not right. You give these two dollars to him when he comes home."

Well, I put my money away just in case I need it later, but my husband and the boys are so excited they spend all their dollars on oranges and other fruit. Most men buy little presents or things to eat for their women. Many women who stay on board are sick or do not feel good, like me.

Lou Ellen

During the ten-day ocean voyage, Katerina described how the passengers' moods changed, matching the weather. Whenever the sky turned black and stormy, and the rain swept sideways, the sea responded with undulation, heavy swells, and whitecaps. When stormy weather forced parents and children to seek shelter inside, it was not long before boredom crept up, tempers flared, babies bawled, kids brawled, and pettiness reigned. However, on warm sunny days when white puffball clouds scudded across azure skies and the sea simmered with gentle rolling waves, both children and adults were happy and chatty. Hope and anticipation dominated most adult conversations.

Daily, the promenade deck was jammed with children playing and adults who were reading or relaxing in wooden lounge chairs. Sitting at corner tables, small groups of people played cards and board games or conversed with various persons.

Saturina stopped again in Halifax, Canada, where it off-loaded passengers and cargo. Then on May 17, everyone was awake early and up on the main deck by midmorning. The ship's officer announced the vessel's arrival in the New York harbor. Refugees finally reached the end of the 4,200-mile voyage in their quest for freedom and a new life.

Katerina

I never forget this day. It is about eleven o'clock in the morning. The whole family is out on deck listening to the earsplitting whistles welcome us. When Saturina approaches the dock, flags from different countries flutter from one end of the ship to the other. I rush down below the deck and gather all our belongings and suitcases together. I also check the lock on Costi's wooden chest which is jampacked with our belongings.

Lou Ellen

When the family walked down the gangplank, Katerina heard dockworkers speaking German to an inspector, so she wandered

163

over to them. The inspector quickly looked inside their trunk and suitcases.

Katerina

Even though I speak many languages, I do not speak or understand English. Inside the trunk is flour, sugar, and some baking items. I also bring along enamel pots and pans, a few bowls, and a couple of mixing spoons. I do not want the inspector seizing any of our possessions, so I speak to him in German and practically beg him not to remove a single thing. I need it all for feeding my husband and five kids, I say. "Oh, don't worry, lady," he assures me. "I won't confiscate a thing." Thank goodness, he keeps his word.

Lou Ellen

Other refugees, standing on the dock, appeared puzzled or confused hearing Katerina speaking German. They asked for her help translating from their languages into German. Katerina replied that she was very sorry, but she could not assist them. She was not feeling well, she explained in a weak voice.

Katerina

Coming off the ship with the rest of us is a German man who struts back and forth on the dock, acting like a king or a hoity-to-ity rich man. He comes to me and asks, "Why don't you want to help people?" I feel like saying that it is none of your business, you dumb jerk. You speak German, so why don't you help them? Instead, I explain that the whole time I am on Saturina, I throw up, and that I can hardly crawl out of bed when I need the toilet. I do not want to say I am pregnant. He pipes up again. "Well, how about your older girl or boy? Can either one translate?" This guy does not give up. He is ticking me off. "None of my kids speak German," I snap. "My kids only speak Italian."

He sends me a dirty look as though I am lying. "Okay, then, forget it," he says. Then he asks me something else. I forget now what. Finally, I say that he wants to know way too much of my business. "Mister," I say, "why don't you learn a brand-new language? It might do you some good."

One of those German dockworkers who is listening to everything going on says to me, "Boy, you cut his pecker good. Now he will have a little bitty one." He laughs so hard he holds his sides. He tells me not to worry over nothing. "I will put you and your family on the proper train that will take you to your destination."

Lou Ellen

The Good Samaritan climbed aboard a waiting bus along with Katerina and her family. When other refugees entered the vehicle and all their belongings were loaded, the driver headed out to the train station. Along the way, the new arrivals marveled at the number of automobiles and tall buildings.

Katerina

What a nice man! He makes sure we get on the proper train and then watches while all our baggage is stored in the rear car. He wishes us good luck and then goes on helping other people. I will always remember him. My husband remarks that this man is one of the very few kind Germans still left in the world. I disagree. I believe there are many more than we can imagine.

After we settle on the train, the conductor comes along and explains that it takes one and a half days of travel before we reach Milltown. The tags we wear around our necks with our pictures give our destination as Milltown, Michigan. I ask Costi where this Michigan place is. "You are always questioning me on something," he says, irritated. "Ask the conductor." I keep nagging him. I am very curious. "Okay, okay," he finally says. "On the ship, the deckhand explains that Michigan is one of the forty-eight states that make up America, also called the United States. They are the same." He adds that Michigan is in a region called the Midwest. Look at this map. "See. Here is Michigan. It looks like a little kid's mitten. Milltown is down here, near the bottom. Are you satisfied now?"

Before long, my husband and the kids sleep practically the whole trip. The rocking back and forth makes them doze off probably. Not me, though. I no can even take a little snooze because I am too excited and nervous. All I can think of is how much longer? Milltown. Here we come!

Milltown

Lou Ellen

It was May 18, 1959, and midday when the train arrived at the Milltown station. The weather turned hot and humid with the temperature already 79 degrees Fahrenheit, unusually warm for that month in southwest Michigan.

Katerina, Costi, and their four children, climbed down from the train. Nearby, a fiftyish-looking couple greeted them with a large hand-printed sign in black letters. It read "Welcome, Marku family." All parties smiled at each other. The American couple spoke so rapidly, neither Katerina nor her husband understood a word they uttered. The couple may be speaking gibberish as far as Katerina understood. Costi offered no help either, as his native tongue was Romanian. He spoke Italian, some Hungarian, and a little English. The children spoke Italian fluently and more English than both their parents could do so together. Apparently, European educators believed it was vital that English language classes should begin at early grade levels.

Following several futile attempts at communication, the church couple retrieved the family's heavy belongings and motioned for them to follow.

Katerina

Once we settle down inside the long roomy vehicle and head away from the station, the woman from church stares at her small German-language book. She flips its pages back and forth many times. Finally, she holds the open book up for us to see and points to the word *haus*. With the book back in her lap, she licks her finger and flips pages again and again. We wait. Finally, she whips around in the front seat, flashes a wide smile, hands me the book, and says, "strasse" then "Belmont." I do not understand what she is trying to tell us. I do know what *strasse* is. I say nothing but am doing plenty of thinking. Who chooses a person who cannot speak or understand a word of German? There must be at least a few German-speaking people in a town this size. Costi doesn't open his mouth either. He is slouched in the seat, half-asleep. Our other kids, exhausted from the train ride, are either nodding off or sleeping. Only curious Gregorio is wide-awake and jiggling with excitement. He pipes up speaking Italian, saying, "Momma! I think the church lady is telling us we are going to our American house." I nod and reply—in Italian—that we probably will stop somewhere on Belmont Street.

Lou Ellen

The two-story white home was located at the southeast section of town within a diverse neighborhood consisting mainly of Hispanics, Blacks, and working class white folks. Two houses away stood an old, abandoned gas station. Nearby, St. Rafael's Catholic Church and school filled an entire block. A small neighborhood market was within easy walking distance from the Marku home.

When their benefactors departed, the children were anxious to investigate their surroundings. Gregorio and Valentina sought their mother's permission to run upstairs and select their own sleeping rooms. Katerina gave her okay. Six-year-old Rosa and her brother Gabi, four, hung back, fearful of climbing the steep staircase.

Katerina

Our kids know respect. They do not run around and do as they please. Beaming with energy, Gregorio bursts upstairs, but before he can climb any more steps, Costi grabs his shirt. "Hey, boy," he yells. "Just where the hell do you think you are going?"

"Ah, Mom says we—"

My husband cuts Gregorio off and attacks me, saying, "Your momma forgets who the boss of this family is. I make the decisions in this house. I choose your bedrooms."

Lou Ellen

Her husband's outburst and hurtful remarks were no surprise, acknowledged Katerina, because he was short on patience and long on criticizing her and the children. Still, she hoped he would ease up a little and relax, now that they would probably face many challenges in their new surroundings. Furthermore, she said she felt like kicking herself, attempting peace in the family by overlooking his faults and remaining silent ever since their marriage. She also confided that she shielded and defended the children each time he swore and humiliated them. Instead, she should have chewed him out, threatened divorce, or called the cops on him if he did not stop such behavior. Costi's conduct frightened and worried her, but she swept her feelings in the corners of her mind. For at that moment, her priority was feeding her hungry family. She needed to buy food.

Katerina

Before the church couple leaves us, I ask if there is a store close by where I can buy food. She mumbles something and shrugs her shoulders. Later, I go for a walk, not far from the Catholic church. In no time, I find a little market. I have two dollars with me, the same two dollars the priest gave me before we left Italy. During our ship layover in Gibraltar, Costi and the kids blew all the money the priest gave them.

Inside the shop, I look around, but I do not say a word since I speak very little English. I pick up a few potatoes, a loaf of bread, milk, and butter. I give the man behind the counter my two dollars. He hands back one penny. I come home and make supper. We have potato soup, bread and butter. By the way, I still have my special penny after all these years, but I cannot find it.

*　　*　　*

At first, Gregorio and Valentina have a hard time in school. Their classmates tease, play jokes, and disrespect them because they speak with heavy accents, wear different-looking European clothes and strange shoes with pointed toes. I tell you what. Americans do not appreciate people who look different or speak another language besides English.

* * *

Lou Ellen

When Katerina dredged up enough nerve to inform her husband that she was again pregnant, Costi, as she had anticipated, was not thrilled with the news. After he thought the matter over, he said to her, "We can probably manage, but we'll have to watch where every dollar we make goes."

Six months later, the Marku family welcomed their fifth child, an easy-to-care-for boy the couple named Roman. When the baby was four months old, Katerina accepted a job cleaning an attorney's office five nights a week. Meanwhile, Costi had been working days at a large garden center in Milltown. His duties included planting flowers, pulling weeds, cutting grass, and acting as a gofer for other employees. His pay was eighty-five cents an hour. Subsequently, her husband worked for an Italian neighbor who started his own painting business taking on small projects such as picket fences, garages, window frames, and inside trim and walls. For that work, Costi was paid $2.50 an hour. While working with the Italian, Costi was introduced to Karoly, another painter, who he learned was employed by the Milltown public school system.

Katerina

As it turns out, Karoly, a Hungarian, and my husband have a lot in common. They hit it off right away. A single man, he immigrated to the United States more than five years ago and speaks very good English. He finds out who the Marku kids are at school and tells them he will help their father land a job in the middle school. They come home all happy and excited, but I tell Costi and the kids to hang on and wait until we know for sure. We do not hear a peep out of anybody for more than two weeks. Costi mopes around the house like a sick pup. Then, out of the blue, Karoly informs Costi he will introduce him to Mr. Buck Weaver, the school principal, who is conducting interviews with candidates seeking employment.

Costi's big day arrives the next morning. Karoly goes along with my husband to the office and first introduces him to what his Hungarian friend describes as the "sexy chick in the short skirt who keeps the books." Next, my husband meets the principal, who asks Karoly to stick around just in case Costi doesn't understand what is being said in English. If Costi needs his help, Karoly can interpret the sentence in Hungarian or Romanian since each one is familiar with both languages.

Well, before I go on, Costi describes Mr. Buck Weaver as a tall, cross-looking man with a flattop haircut. He asks my husband if he has experience at painting and other minor repairs. Costi says in the summertime, he and an Italian friend work as a team painting inside and outside many homes in the area, and they keep busy with other similar projects. Costi explains to Mr. Weaver that anyone who wants work as a painter or paperhanger in Italy, is required to attend classes where he learns different kinds of paint, working with proper tools, and how to use safety equipment, for example. At this point, my husband says he pulls out his technical school diploma, showing that he passed many practical exams and met all the other requirements. Then he hands the certificate over to Mr. Buck Weaver so he can look it over.

Now when my husband comes to this part of the story, he nearly croaks laughing. He describes how Mr. Weaver grabs his spectacles, puts them on, and proceeds reading the document line by line. All along, he nods his head, moves his lips like he is reading and understanding every single word, and then hands it back. "Can you believe it?" my husband says. "Every single word is written in Italian." After Costi catches his breath and stops laughing, he continues, saying, "At this point, I am dying to ask Mr. Weaver where he learned such good Italian." While Costi doubts whether he should ask the question or not, he says he blurts out, "In America, Mr. Weaver, it looks

171

like anybody who owns a brush and a gallon of paint can find work as a painter. This never happens in Italy." In a flash, Costi says, Mr. Weaver passes the diploma back. Now my husband is positive he messed up the interview and any chance he had for a new job. Much to his surprise, Mr. Buck Weaver shakes his hand and says, "Well, Mr. Marku. I am very impressed with your qualifications. It looks like you are the right man for this position. Congratulations, Costi. Welcome aboard."

Lou Ellen

Looking back, Katerina said Costi's first day on the job was "a real bitch," as he described it. His two paint shop coworkers were supposed to work with him at the elementary school building. After lunch break, Costi explained, Karoly and another painter explained that they needed to pick up tools at another building and added, "We'll be back in a jiffy. See you later." Instead, the men showed up at 2:30 p.m. smelling like a brewery.

Katerina

These birdbrains never tell Costi what to do. Instead of waiting for them to come back, my husband finishes painting the remaining two walls by himself. Karoly, the Hungarian who helps him land the job, says to Costi, "You dumb dago. Don't work so hard. Paint a little, then sit down and rest."

My husband's answer is, "Listen. When somebody puts me to work, I do it." Costi goes on to explain that in Italy, painters never leave job sites until their assignments are finished, not before. Also, he gripes that he didn't expect working alone, especially the first day. Making matters worse, Costi criticizes his coworkers' work habits and praises their Italian counterparts. "In Italy," he says, "painters take pride in their work, and they work as a team. But then, this is something you guys are not familiar with, I guess."

When my upset husband blurts out with this gem, Karoly apologizes for calling him a dago and swears he will never "pull a stupid stunt like this again." The second guy, tipsy brave, is mad as a charging bull. Costi says he swears like a pickled sailor and asks him if his pea brain tells him he lives in "the good ol' USA, and to hell with Italy."

Lou Ellen

The following day, Katerina learned that Costi did not eat during noontime break. When he opened his lunch pail, he discovered a dead mouse. The culprit was the angry worker who believed his prank was hilarious. After she hears her husband's story, Katerina grabbed her son Gregorio to stand by in case she required assistance with English while she telephoned the school office. She lodged her complaint and identified the angry painter as "that painter guy with a gold front tooth who thinks playing tricks on people is funny."

Katerina

It takes some time, but the school winds up firing him. He has many complaints against him, I learn. I add one more. In time, a new part-time worker is hired. According to my husband, the new man works mostly as a janitor but fills in as a painter when he is needed. Teachers especially like the new janitor because is friendly and takes great pains sweeping and mopping classroom floors, changing light bulbs, or making minor repairs. When teachers ask for help, he drops everything at once and meets their requests.

For the most part, life at the middle school sails along as normal until classes resume following spring break. Suddenly, teachers, the principal, office workers—the whole school—is in an uproar. It seems the gym teacher catches the favored janitor with a scrub bucket in the girl's restroom, peeking through the gap in a stall door with a girl inside. Well, following an investigation and his admission of guilt, the school fired his fanny at once. I find it strange that Milltown schools hire so many creeps.

*　　*　　*

Lou Ellen

As the five children grow older and more independent, Katerina obtained a new position working in the elementary school cafeteria. Gradually she learned and understood more and more English. Communicating with others became easier. Nevertheless, she continued relying on the older children for learning words she did not understand. Consequently, she consulted her trusty dictionary for correct spellings and usage.

Katerina

Every day, I learn more English, but with five kids and a husband to take care of, I do not have time or energy to take language classes. I pretty much understand what people say, but I do not talk the proper way, I know.

* * *

In 1961, two years after we left Europe, two men in dark suits wearing badges, come to the house. I do not know if they are police, FBI, or what; they don't say but show us their US government identification cards. Anyway, the two show Costi and me a photograph. They ask us if we know this man. "Yah," I say. "I think I know him. I remember translating his immigration papers at Camp Salerno."

One man says, "You what? Are you absolutely certain, Mrs. Marku?"

I explain to him. I translate for many people there, and yes, I am sure he is the same guy. His young partner pipes up, saying, "You were not authorized to assist him. Are you aware of that?" His question catches me off guard.

Who tells me this? I say nobody does. "Back there, I translate for hundreds who want to enter different countries. Why should I refuse to help him? I know nothing about him. All I know is the camp police sends him to the consulate first, and if he answers their questions, and they believe his answers, he is okay. Then they send him back to me."

He sighs, then goes on. "Well, my good lady. Something is very wrong, but we will get to the bottom of it. I guarantee." I agree, then ask why he comes here instead of going back to the consulate in Naples. "Ask them," I say, getting upset.

"Do not yell on me! If you keep hollering, I'm warning you that I will poke you good in the eye. You are not polite. You show me no respect. I will not talk to you anymore."

The quiet man with gray hair who does not say a word the whole time just looks at my wood floor. The mouthy young one opens his yap again, but his partner butts in, saying, "Stop. Stop right now, Chad. You say enough."

By now, I am steaming like a boiling kettle. I do not know these two men from Adam. They might be crooks or shysters for all I know. They flash their badges, practically barge their selves inside my house, and start pumping us for information.

The silent partner finally speaks up. "Ma'am, we apologize. My young partner here is still in training. He thinks he can do and say anything he wants. He has much more to learn. I apologize for us both."

I look at him right in the eye. "Sir, I say, I will tell you something. I work with so many people my whole life, and I never see such a cock-a-poo like him—ever." He understands what I am saying, and he agrees. He suggests that smart aleck Chad "step outside with Mr. Marku for a few minutes and take a break."

Once the two are outside, the gentleman sits with me at the kitchen table and makes small talk. Then he laughs. "You certainly cleaned his clock. Mrs. Marku, you fixed him good. You even warned Chad about poking his eye out. I know you would. You were that close." He makes a small space between his thumb and first finger. "I will say this, Mrs. Katerina Marku. You are a real fighter."

He is exactly right. All my life, I am a fighter, or I be dead by now, for sure. You also must use your head and be smart. If you don't think before you open your mouth, this can be a death sentence.

Lou Ellen

For the next several years, Katerina and Costi rented the home on Belmont Street, and eventually they became citizens of the United States. When school ended for summer vacation, the couple earned extra money painting houses with their Hungarian friend. Katerina painted trim and windows. The two men tackled ceilings and entire rooms. Gradually the Marku's saved enough funds to purchase their own home. It was located two blocks from their rental place within a similar diverse neighborhood.

Katerina joined the Parent-Teacher Association in the children's school and accepted room mother responsibilities for several of their younger children. She also labored at the Salvation Army twice a week sorting incoming donations. In addition, she volunteered her spare time and effort for an up-and-coming young politician who was running for election to the Michigan State Legislature. Her home oftentimes served as a gathering place for many parties and other fund-raising opportunities for her popular Democratic friend.

The couple also joined the European Club in town where they made many new friends. The organization gathered monthly, and on special occasions, it sponsored dances, musical groups, and held other social activities. Many members were transplants from war-torn European countries.

Oftentimes, during those meetings, Katerina noticed that two flirtatious women enjoyed teasing and putting their hands on Costi. He relished their attention and playfulness. She also realized her husband was drinking an increasing number of his favorite boilermakers (whiskey and beer). She said she attempted discussing those concerns with him after the children were asleep, but he flew off the handle and accused her of being jealous. He berated her for interfering in his life.

Meanwhile, Katerina continued attending the nondenominational church in Milltown. She believed it was an obligation that she must fulfill; after all, the church sponsored the family that enabled them to enter the United States, and they provided housing, furnishings, and other assistance. Nevertheless, following Katerina's recovery from a flu-like illness, she had a change of heart and quit attending Peaceful Valley Church.

Katerina

I miss church for two weeks straight, so the minister comes to the house with his wife one Sunday afternoon. I am over the virus infection, so now I am busy mending socks. The kids are outdoors playing. We all go in the backyard and sit at the picnic table. I pass around ice tea. Well, we chat about different things awhile, and I say, "You know what, Reverend? No offense, but I no can come to your church anymore. I no can pray with my rosary. I am Catholic through and through. I am sorry."

By now, Costi is smoking like a Turk and not saying a word. The minister assures me he understands. His wife agrees. My husband's preference is Greek Orthodox. He never goes to church with me, and he does not want it. By the way, not a single Greek Orthodox Church is in Milltown or anywhere else nearby. Once in a great while, Costi will visit the Orthodox church in a small town near Lake Michigan. It is more than thirty-five miles away. He likes the Russian priest there.

Now back to my story. The minister goes on to say, "I can see you are not comfortable worshipping at our church. This is perfectly all right, Katerina. It is your choice." Finally, I find enough courage and blurt out that I'm sorry, but from now on, I am worshipping at St. Rafael Catholic Church.

Lou Ellen

Again, the pastor reassured Katerina he was fine with her decision and added if her family ever needed anything, he and his entire congregation stood ready to assist them. At once, Katerina felt her Lord lifting a heavy block from her back, she explained, and she was most grateful. Her contentment, however, was short-lived.

The following week, two women from the Peaceful Valley Church called on Katerina, explaining that they belonged to the Sunshine Committee. "We routinely call on members of the congregation and others who attend our services regularly," the reed-thin woman explained. Her eyes circled the living room before she focused on Katerina.

"Yes," her companion emphasized. "The past few weeks, you have not been in church. We are concerned. Is there a reason you have stopped coming? Is there anything we can do to bring you back into the fold?"

Katerina

I cannot go to your church anymore, I explain. I am Catholic since I'm a little girl, and I belong to St. Rafael's Church now. Suddenly, the skinny woman gets all excited and jabs her finger at me. She yells and says if I do not go to church, I will burn in hell. I ask her nice to stop yelling, please. Once more, she warns that I will go straight to hell. Straight out, I tell her she will go first. "Oh no," she answers. "I am faithful. I attend every Sunday unless I am ill."

By this time, I am fuming. "Do you call yourself a Christian? Where is your kindness and understanding, huh?" Before she can say another word, I make clear she has no right coming here and criticizing me. Besides, where I attend church is a personal choice, nobody else's.

Still boiling inside, and admitting I'm running out of patience, I have half a notion to grab her and slap her silly. "My door is open," I say. "Get out and don't come back."

She says something under her nose. I don't hear what she is saying. Again, I order her out.

The other woman does not say a word, but grabs Skinny by the arm, and they leave. A few days go by when the nice lady comes back and apologizes. She takes my hand and in a soft silky voice says, "You know, Katerina. I had no idea how nasty she is. For heaven's sake, I will never pressure anyone about attending church. Instead of setting a good example, her actions do nothing but turn people off. Each person must make his own decision regarding spiritual matters. Again, I am terribly sorry."

I accept her apology and thank her for smoothing everything over. Even so, I cannot forget—even after all these years.

Aftermath

Katerina

Honestly, I never shared my experiences with Polish friends here in Milltown, and they kept quiet about theirs. Back then, people avoided talking about such horrible things. In fact, I do not remember ever bringing the subject up with my second husband or the children, either. The rule in this household was what you hear in your home stays right here. You say nothing to nobody else.

Costi never talked much about his family in Romania. I knew he had a daughter before he was a soldier fighting along the front. He told me about her back when we were in the displacement camp at Mercatello, Italy. I almost called it quits with him right then. In later years, Costi hoped they would meet each other some day.

All I ever knew about his parents were the little bits he told me after he had been swilling down too many boilermakers (beer and whiskey). He said that a comrade came from the city and informed him that both his mother and father were blindfolded, shot, and killed in the village square. I never knew who did this, or why. Costi always blamed Russian soldiers. Sometime later, he said after fighting in Yugoslavia, he threw down his weapons and wound up working in the coal mines. From there, he moved on to Italy and landed in a refugee camp where I first met him.

As I look back on my life as a kid growing up, being forced to work for the Nazis in Dachau, and living in the many refugee camps, I believe these experiences made me hard and tough. I am convinced that if my mother had not died when she did, I would have had a very different life. I wouldn't have been mistreated, beaten, and chased away, or called bad names. My stepmother, Michalina, pushed me around so many times, I began feeling like a useless threadbare dustrag that should be thrown away. Being a young girl, I cried constantly because I never understood what I had done wrong or why she didn't like me. On the other hand, she treated her kids like gold while I was worth cock-a-poo in her eyes. As I grew up and understood circumstances better, I no longer cried. Even so, strangers frightened me, and I had a hard time trusting anyone, even friends. Also, if anyone raised his voice, I trembled like an aspen leaf—just as I did so often at Dachau.

Although we are now citizens and have been living in the United States for many years, I always check out my surroundings. I constantly glance over my shoulder, making sure I am safe. This does not happen as often anymore, but I always keep my guard up. Even today, if a stranger stops me on the street and asks questions, I always look at him straight in the eye. If he looks down toward the ground, I ignore his questions, figuring he is not sincere. I make an excuse and walk away.

As I mentioned earlier, Milltown school was not a happy experience at first for Gregorio and Valentina. The teachers placed Gregorio in the sixth grade instead of the eighth grade, where he belonged. They thought he needed time adjusting to his new life. Because Valentina and Gregorio talked with heavy accents and dressed differently, kids teased and disrespected them. Even so, it wasn't long before the opposite happened. Gregorio took up baseball, got into football and became a good athlete. Suddenly, his classmates accepted him, and he made many friends. Valentina had such a good heart; she became pals with a lonely mute girl in her class. Her classroom teacher used Valentina's kindness as an example for her classmates to follow. Her instructor stressed how important it was for everyone to treat others as they would like to be treated, and ignore all differences. The students paid attention to their teacher. In no time, the teasing stopped; classmates, both boys and girls, warmed up to her, and she wound up with many chums.

For me, the first few years living in America were very disturbing, especially when World War II films about Hitler, his SS troops, and their shocking actions came on TV. I could not watch then, and I cannot look at them now, except for a few minutes. It is such a shame. So many young men die in war; it tears me up inside.

When war stories come on television, and I watch more than a few minutes, I start shaking. Then I sit down and say a prayer because I relive the misery all over again.

Since my kids are all grown up now, they are constantly dishing out advice, saying, "Mom. When WW II battles are shown on TV, just find another station or else hit the power off button." When my daughter-in-law (Gregorio's wife) visits, and sees me upset, she asks, "What were you watching, Mom? A program about World War II?" It just came on, I explain, but she loses patience, and grumbles, "Just don't watch while you are sitting here alone. Wait until you have a friend over or a visitor. Then when the program ends, you and the other person can talk over what you have seen—only if you initiate it first."

The worst part comes at night when I am home alone, and the evening news comes on television. More often than not, a war or conflict is going on somewhere in the world, and the report always shows young soldiers in battle. When this happens, I walk from room to room, just as if a firecracker exploded nearby. I no can sit or settle down. Then around 2:00 a.m., I toss and turn for what seems like hours. I no can fall asleep. When I finally drift off, I wake up sweating and crying like a baby. The dream never changes. I am running from a grizzly guard in Dachau who chases me, shoots, drags my body, and stuffs me into a blazing furnace. This is my war, and I do not like it.

Another thing bothers me. In every war, many young soldiers come home crippled or with messed-up minds. I don't like saying this, but Americans do not take care of their veterans, as they should. This is not right. These men are hungry, sick, and sleeping out on the streets. All vets need good jobs. Why, I find five or six letters every week in my mailbox, asking me for money. I used to help while I was working, but no more. Now I spend too much money for medicine.

This is what war does to our brave young men, but I am little. What can I do? Nothing.

In fact, my living and surviving in wartime affected me emotionally for many years. In other words, my heart was overflowing with hate for Germans, especially the Nazis and the death squads; they had no feeling or no mercy for any other human beings on earth. I imagine these men could have lived as ordinary people, but Hitler deceived them and let power go to his head. Still, I cannot understand why many German citizens either ignored what was happening in their country at that time or closed their eyes and ignored it.

In my opinion, every person who shot, killed, tortured, and burned innocent humans was sick, evil, or both. In the beginning, there was no way on God's earth that I could ever forgive these people. What I never realized at the time was all that hate I carried inside was eating me up alive. I think I might have gone crazy, though, if Father Finnegan at St. Rafael Catholic Church had not stepped in. One day, he gave me a good raking over when he said, "Katerina, my dear lady. You have so much hate baggage you are carrying around, you must drop it and let it go. If you ignore my advice and do nothing, I guarantee, it will destroy you. You need to raise your children wisely and not pass on to them your hostility and loathing."

Father Finnegan told me this a long time ago. It took years before I followed his advice. And it wasn't easy by a long shot. In fact, I no longer have bad feelings toward German people as I once did because I believe hate is wrong; it is a mortal sin.

Besides, I am certain that the constant pain and worry over whether I would live or die in Dachau, and the hardships experienced during the war, affected the way Costi and I raised our kids. For one thing, we did not put up with any foolishness, like begging or whining for things we could not afford. We also insisted they behave properly, use good manners, and be polite. I remember we constantly pounded into their heads the importance of respecting every human being and care less about language, skin color, or lifestyle.

I realize now that my husband was especially tough with the children. In his mind, the kids never did anything right. Matter of fact, I never did anything that satisfied him, either. He was forever telling me what to do. Honestly, living with Costi was not easy, but the kids and I managed.

As I explained to Lou Ellen at the beginning, the main reason I am telling my story now is that I am an old woman. Some young people think it is smart when they call old folks Q-tips because we have white hair. I could care less. In fact, I have been called worse names in my life, and like most folks my age, I don't give a rat's arse what anybody thinks.

The second reason for telling my story is that even now, there are people who do not believe the Nazis killed or tortured the Poles, Jews, homosexuals, and gypsies—or anyone else who did not fit Hitler's theory that people with blue eyes, blond hair, and total German blood equals a pure race. I am familiar with a few of these denying types. They belong to the European Club that Costi and I were once members of. All the photos, real-life movies, witnesses, and trials make no difference to them. They insist that so-called murderous acts are "simply American government propaganda." I do not bother arguing with them anymore. They do not listen to what I say, so why waste my breath? I lived through it. I know the truth.

I believe with all my heart that the world must never forget Hitler and World War II. It is the duty of people like me who lived through the war to tell our personal stories. If we keep these memories to ourselves and die, they are lost forever. Every generation needs reminders of man's inhumanity to his fellow man and the futility of war. We owe this much to the millions of people who died: soldiers from all parts of Europe and America; plain, hard-working men and women (forced workers) who were starved, tortured, shot, or committed suicide. Every one made a sacrifice for us who live. They made possible our freedom and independence. It is sad, I know, but most Americans I know do not appreciate or even think about freedom; they take it for granted.

Epilogue

Lou Ellen

Today, my cherished friend, the real-life Katerina, is ninety-three years old. She continues living in the same home in which she and Costi purchased and raised their five children. The couple reunited with his Romanian daughter, Zena. She visited her father after more than twenty-six years of separation. She married and had one son. At the time, she worked in Romania as a laboratory technician.

Costi, a thirty-year Milltown Public School employee who worked in the painting and maintenance department, died from heart disease a few months prior to his sixtieth birthday. Katerina relied on Father Finnegan at St. Rafael's Church for helping her cope with the loss.

Katerina

During this period, Father Finnegan came to my rescue. He helped me keep sane. When Costi died, Father came to the house, talked with me, and explained that life is just like the weather. He said, "Today it is very nice outdoors, warm and sunny. Tomorrow it will rain, and there will be lightning and thunder. This is the same way as life. You go to work, you come home, and the next morning, your loved one is gone. You see, this is what happens. Your life at that moment was like a big storm with thunder, lightning, and powerful winds." I will never forget his words.

Lou Ellen

Following the death of her husband, Katerina enlisted the help of her daughter-in-law (Gregorio's wife) for help in sending a telegram to his Romanian daughter.

Katerina

We thought she would want to know her father died, but we waited for some word from her. Weeks went by. Nothing. Finally, my daughter-in-law checked with Western Union. As it turned out, the message was delivered, and his daughter signed it. Unbelievable. Nobody from Romania wrote or even telephoned. Here my husband was sending her one hundred dollars each month. Wouldn't you think she would send a card or a little note? My husband has been gone for more than twenty-five years now, and I have never heard one word. After Costi passed, I did not send her one red cent, either.

Lou Ellen

A widow for a quarter century, Katerina continues living alone in her home, performing household chores without help and cooking for herself. Recently, her everyday tasks take more time and energy since she currently relies on a walker to move around the house. In addition, she required oxygen for labored breathing due to asthma.

In earlier years, Katerina treated her children and grandchildren with stuffed cabbage rolls, rosettes (deep-fried cookies), and other Polish baked goods. However, she no longer is physically able to duplicate those goodies today. Nevertheless, with help from family members and a friendly Hispanic neighbor, Katerina still tends and enjoys her many perennial flowers. The neighbor tends her vegetable garden regularly and shares part of the bounty with her.

Additionally, she continues collecting cast-off clothing from friends and acquaintances, then gives several grocery bags filled with donations to the St. Rafael Church outreach committee. That organization distributes such donations to needy families in the community. Furthermore, Katerina knits more than thirty pair of mittens, scarves, and hats annually for her church bazaar, whose proceeds are used for benevolent parish projects.

Her firstborn son, Gregorio, became an educated, hard-working, respected member of the Milltown community. Early in his adult life, he had a variety of interests and jobs. At times, he painted houses and garages, laid tile, and became a chef. Later, he joined the International Brotherhood of Electrical Workers Union and served as a union organizer for many years. He also became a member of the Masonic lodge. Subsequently, he married his high school sweetheart, and the couple had four sons. Two of them are twins. Together, the family engaged in several sports and outdoor activities, including golf, canoeing, hunting, and fishing, along with traveling around the country.

Suddenly, tragedy struck the household. Gregorio was diagnosed with a gradual debilitating disease, and he died at age sixty-three.

Katerina's remaining four children attended or graduated from college, held good jobs, and had children. All of them are productive members of their communities. At present, the family circle has grown to include nine grandchildren (eight boys and one girl) and eighteen great-grandchildren.

At one point in her life, Katerina sent a letter to the parish priest in Horodenka, Poland, to inquire about the status of her rightful inheritance, her parents' home.

Katerina

I asked if the house is still standing. If it is, I wanted to know if someone is living there. I put ten dollars in the envelope to pay for his time, trouble, and postage. I heard nothing. I know the priest got my letter; it never came back.

Oh well. I must live in the present. If I think about my childhood and experiences as a young person, I no can sleep or eat. Instead, I will sit, pout, and wind up sick. It is all behind me now. I believe that the Lord and his angels have been looking out for me most of my life, so I thank Him. I give thanks for keeping me safe in the evening before I fall asleep and every morning when I open my eyes. I believe very much in the healing power of prayer and forgiveness.

Miracles? I believe in them too. Remember the fine handmade gloves the doctor's wife, Gerta, gave me in Stuttgart? Well, for years and years, I stored them for safekeeping in the house; I no remembered where. Every year I hunted for them. I began thinking the kids played with them, or my husband got mad at me and pitched them out. I thought my special gloves were gone for good. Then of all things, one bright sunny day, I was in the mood to go through piles of old letters and papers before tossing the stuff out, and what did I find? My beautiful tan-color gloves. As I rubbed my hands all over them, they were still soft as baby skin. Each stich and every tiny white-pearl button was still in place. It is hard to believe that after seventy years, they kept their beauty. These gloves are precious. They remind me that there is always something fine and good, even in the middle of death and destruction.

I sincerely hope that no person who reads my story will ever forget the millions of innocent men, women, and children who died terrible deaths. Those poor souls never had a chance. What an awful waste.

Afterword

Lou Ellen

As a freelance writer and photographer for area magazines and other publications, I am especially on the lookout for unique human-interest stories. It was during a routine office visit with my family physician that I first heard Katerina's name. He mentioned he had an elderly patient who spent time in Dachau as a forced worker during WWII and wanted to know if I was interested in meeting her, possibly leading to a new writing project. On several occasions, he had given me leads on other pieces. Our family physician knew little about her personal life, he added, except that she was Polish.

Immediately, my internal antennae shot up. I had visited Dachau many years earlier. At the time, I lived on the German economy in Bad Nauheim with my soldier husband. We managed to travel on a limited budget, thanks to cut-rate GI tour packages. The concentration/forced worker camp in Dachau with its barbed wire, brick crematorium, and personal exhibits was heart-wrenching and emotionally draining. Other stops on the tour included Hitler's mountain bunker, Rommel's grave, and American war memorial locations in several countries.

Without delay, I answered Dr. Xavier's question. "Certainly," I told him. "I can hardly wait to meet this woman and listen to her narrative if she is willing to share it with me, a complete stranger." I wondered, would she trust me enough to reveal her horrible experiences, thoughts, and emotions during wartime?

Meanwhile, several weeks passed, and I heard nothing further. Then the doctor's nurse phoned and gave me Katerina's full name, home address, and her telephone number. However, before I hauled out my Canon camera and tape recorder for the interview, it seemed wise that I call her, introduce myself, and engage in a little small talk. If that went well, I would arrange a home visit. The first attempt at contacting her failed. The telephone rang many times. Finally, she picked up. Then without a word spoken on either end, the line clicked dead. That was puzzling. I made two more attempts to call and met the same result.

Back at Dr. Xavier's office several weeks later, I mentioned my difficulty contacting Katerina. I said to the physician, "I guess Katerina changed her mind. She hangs up on me before I can utter a word." Apparently, he gave her a hefty dose of persuasion, for when I made a final try at phoning her, Katerina answered. We set a date for our first get-acquainted meeting at her home.

Subsequently, for four years, I listened, emphasized, recorded, and transcribed her narrative. Knowing that her wartime experiences occurred more than a half-century ago. I understood Katerina's failure at recalling specific details, descriptions of persons, and some situations that were vague or forgotten. In such cases, I have taken creative liberties with some scenes and descriptions of persons and their individual characteristics.

Additionally, Katerina's name, as well as family members, friends, and others depicted in the story, have been altered for identity protection and privacy. The actual American city, in which she currently lives, as well as the church and school, are fictitious.

Furthermore, it is true that both Katerina I were patients of the same physician. At present, he teaches medical school students as well as continuing a private practice. Katerina is among his patients.

I continue visiting Katerina on a regular basis as she and I have become very good friends. In addition, her inspiring story demonstrates that every human being who has strength, courage, and faith can survive even the most horrendous circumstances.

Glossary

Allied Forces. The big four allied powers of World War II were the United Kingdom, the United States of America, France, and the Soviet Union, along with many other nations, from 1939 to 1945.

Autobahn. The German expressway, which has no general speed limit, but some hilly and construction areas may have temporary or conditional limits.

Babushka.-A woman's scarf, oftentimes triangular and worn over the head, usually ties under the chin.

Concentration camp. After WWII began in 1939, concentration camps became places where millions of ordinary people are confined as part of the war effort. They are starved, tortured, and killed. During the war, thousands of new concentration camps and sub-camps for Hitler's "undesirable" people opened throughout occupied Europe.

DP/Displaced Person camp. A temporary facility for housing displaced persons forced into migration.

Eastern front. It is among the largest military battles in history. It encompassed Central and Eastern Europe from 1941 to 1945. During four years, more than four hundred Red Army and German divisions fought in many operations extending more than one thousand miles. This resulted in the destruction and partition of Nazi Germany, the rise of the Soviet Union as a subpower, and its occupation of Eastern Europe.

Forced/Slave laborers. Civilians, prisoners, deportees, foreign nationals, Jews, and prisoners of war coerced into the labor system that covered most of Europe; it supported the war efforts of the Nazi regime and Axis countries. Workers built roads, constructed buildings, labored in mines and munition factories and various other industries.

Heinrich Himmler. A Nazi politician, police administrator, and military commander who was the second most powerful man in the Third Reich. Men under his command feared him because he committed brutal acts.

Kraut. A derogatory term for German soldiers often used during WWI and WWII.

Menorah. A symbol from the Jewish faith; it is a seven-branched candelabrum with eight candles.

Third Reich. Another term for Nazi Germany when Hitler ruled the totalitarian state.

Western front. Large-scale combat operations Germany initiated against Western countries such as the United Kingdom, France, Belgium, the Netherlands, Luxembourg, and Denmark. There were two phases. In the first phase, Belgium, the Netherlands, and Denmark surrendered during May and June 1940. Then France fell. By that time, Nazi Germany had one major enemy left in Western Europe— Great Britain. Germany expected to conquer Britain quickly, but by October 1940, Britain endured, and Germans postponed their planned sea invasion. The second combat phase included ground troop operations, which began in June 1944, with Allied landings in Normandy, and continued until Germany's defeat in May 1945.

About the Author

Lee Griffin is a graduate of Western Michigan University with a BS degree in education. She is the mother of four adult children and has five grandchildren. Griffin taught elementary physical education in the Kalamazoo public schools and lived in Germany where she and her husband had their first child. Back in the U.S., she began a freelance writing and photography career for the Kalamazoo Gazette, Battle Creek Enquirer and Grand Rapids Press which continued for 26 years. During that time, she received a media award from the Kalamazoo County Education Association for outstanding news reporting in the interest of education. Later, she received an individual artist grant from the Kalamazoo Arts Council which partially funded the writing of her non-fiction book, *Kalamazoo and Southwest Michigan: Golden Memories*. Griffin currently resides with her husband Bob, a retired senior research biologist with Pharmacia and Willy II, a rescued Boxer mix. They live on a nineteen-acre, certified tree farm near the village of Augusta, Michigan.

CPSIA information can be obtained
at www.ICGtesting.com
Printed in the USA
FFOW03n0454120518
46506081-48457FF